ANTI-

INFLAMMATORY

DIET FOR BEGINNERS

COPYRIGHT

Under no circumstances will any legal responsibility or blame be held against the publisher for any reparation, damages, or monetary loss due to the information herein, either directly or indirectly.

Respective authors own all copyrights not held by the publisher.

The information herein is offered for informational purposes solely, and is universal as so. The presentation of the information is without contract or any type of guarantee assurance.

The trademarks that are used are without any consent, and the publication of the trademark is without permission or backing by the trademark owner. All trademarks and brands within this book are for clarifying purposes only and are the owned by the owners themselves, not affiliated with this document

ABOUT THE BOOK

The Anti-Inflammation Diet for Beginners shows you what an anti-inflammatory diet is all about and how it can help you prevent the onset of multiple deadly diseases. The Anti-Inflammatory Diet for Beginner features the overview of the science behind the anti-inflammatory diet and how it can permanently improve your health. With this book, you'll learn how to choose your foods wisely on an anti-inflammatory diet in order to reduce this life-threatening reaction, and get rid of the painful symptoms of inflammation. This book shows you how you can achieve long-lasting health benefits from an anti-inflammatory diet with the 30-day anti-inflammatory diet meal plan containing over 60 simple and nourishing anti-inflammatory diet recipes to help you relieve inflammation symptoms quickly. The book walks you through an effective and complete anti-inflammatory diet with no prior knowledge re□uired. You can learn how to shop for the right ingredients, plan your meals, batch-prep ahead of time, and even use your leftovers for other recipes. Furthermore, it includes 4-week long list of physical activities and exercises that will help you mentally and logistically support your anti-inflammatory diet.

□

TABLE OF CONTENT PAGES

[?]

Introduction

It is becoming increasingly clear that chronic inflammation is the root cause of several serious illnesses – including heart disease, cancers, and Alzheimer's disease. It is very obvious that inflammation on the surface of the body as local redness, heat, swelling and pain. It is the cornerstone of the body's healing response, bringing more nourishment and more immune activity to a site of injury or infection. But when inflammation persists or serves no purpose, it damages the body and causes illness. Stress, lack of exercise, genetic predisposition, and exposure to toxins can all contribute to such chronic inflammation, but dietary choices play a big role as well. Learning how specific foods influence the inflammatory process is the best strategy for containing it and reducing long-term disease risks. The anti-inflammatory diet, and lifestyle management in general, provides an important method of reducing the levels of pain.

Nutrition that supports a diet rich in anti-inflammatory foods is one of the best approach to chronic pain management. The anti-inflammatory diet is a lynchpin of such an integrative approach. The Anti-Inflammatory Diet is not a diet in the popular sense – it is not intended as a weight-loss program although people can and do lose weight on it, nor is the anti-inflammatory diet an eating plan to stay on for a limited period of time. Rather, it is way of selecting and preparing anti-inflammatory foods based on scientific knowledge of how they can help your body maintain optimum health. Along with influencing inflammation, this natural anti-inflammatory diet will provide steady energy and ample vitamins, minerals, essential fatty acids dietary fiber, and protective phytonutrients.

Importantly, this approach to pain management is without any negative side effects. Unpleasant side effects of some medications, including fogginess, memory loss and sleepiness, are no longer a problem. Following the anti-inflammatory diet is a powerful therapy for pain control with many beneficial side effects. The anti-inflammatory diet coupled with physical activities is considered an integrative approach to inflammation.

?

What Is the Anti-Inflammatory Diet?

An anti inflammatory diet is a way of eating that helps reduce chronic inflammation in your body. An anti-inflammatory diet is all about eating more of the foods that help to squash inflammation in the body, while limiting the foods that tend to increase inflammation, thus helping to combat inflammatory conditions. The diet emphasizes lots of colorful fruits and vegetables, high-fiber legumes and whole grains, healthy fats (like those found in salmon, nuts and olive oil) and antioxidant-rich herbs, spices and tea, while limiting processed foods made with unhealthy trans fats, refined carbohydrates (like white flour and added sugar) and too much sodium.

Chronic inflammation in the body can cause serious, long-term health effects, such as heart disease, stroke and arthritis, and make it difficult to lose weight. An anti-inflammatory diet is rich in fruit and vegetables, wholegrains, seafood, nuts and seeds, monounsaturated fatty acids and spices. Similarly, it avoids sugar, processed foods and saturated fats to help reduce inflammation. By following an anti inflammatory diet meal plan and making anti inflammatory recipes, you can reduce symptoms and hopefully heal auto-immune diseases, regulate your cycles, reduce anxiety, bloat and so much more.

Linking Inflammation to Chronic Diseases

Inflammation contributes to the development and symptoms of chronic illnesses, and understanding that link is the first step in knowing how to change your diet in order to combat inflammation and take better care of yourself. Here are some illnesses linked to inflammation:

 Heart Disease

Clinical research has linked heart disease — from coronary artery disease to congestive heart failure — to inflammation. Physicians and researchers provide evidence that the fatty deposits the body uses to repair damage to the arteries are just the start.

 Cancer

Foods and proteins, such as fruits and green vegetables, can help you significantly reduce your risks of cancer. Chronic inflammation has been shown to contribute to the growth of tumor cells and other cancer cells.

Arthritis and Joint Pain

Arthritis has always been linked to inflammation, but it hasn't always been evident that a change in diet could help alleviate the pain and possibly even postpone the onset. Now, however, medical and nutrition professionals see the benefits that natural, vitamin-rich foods can have in relieving the pain of arthritis and possibly even diminishing the inflammation.

Weight Gain

It's no secret that food is linked to obesity, but certain foods have a tendency to pile on the pounds more than others. Refined flours and sugars, for example, don't get digested properly and turn to fat much sooner than other, unprocessed foods. Obesity increases inflammation throughout the body by piling pressure on the joints and aiding arthritis, for instance.

Why is an Anti-Inflammatory Diet Important?

Inflammation is your body's natural reaction as it fights off tissue damage, chemicals, or other injurious elements. Although naturally, a continued state of inflammation may lead to common diseases like diabetes and heart disease. Inflammation can also exacerbate pain among chronic pain sufferers. Incorporating foods that fight inflammation into your diet can keep you healthy and decrease pain. Inflammation is a perpetual component of chronic disease that can be greatly altered through proper dietary intake. Choosing an anti-inflammation diet is one way to control inflammation in your body. For anyone living with chronic inflammation, finding a way to decrease symptoms and, if possible, erase the inflammation altogether, is a blessing. In many cases, living with inflammation doesn't have to be permanent — you can treat, prevent, and sometimes even eradicate those inflammatory issues by knowing which foods are triggers for you, which foods are bad for you, and how to change your diet accordingly. The anti-inflammatory diet isn't one specific diet. It's really a scientifically based way of eating that optimizes your health by bringing more nourishment to the body. The basic premise behind the anti-inflammatory style of eating is simple: When you add nutrients such as fiber, vitamins, minerals, essential fatty acids, and phytonutrients (plant-based compounds) to your meals, you decrease inflammation.

Although all fruits and vegetables contain powerful micronutrients that target your cells and boost your overall health, some foods carry extra anti-inflammatory benefits. An anti-inflammatory diet is based on limiting your body's exposure to foreign antigens while increasing the intake of beneficial nutrients especially nutrients that have anti-inflammatory effects. The general concept of an anti-inflammatory diet are:

1. Reduce processed, refined or manufactured food
2. Eat a variety of brightly colored fruits and vegetables every day.
3. Minimize the intake of saturated fats and eliminate trans fats while increasing good sources of anti-inflammatory fatty acids such as omega-3.
4. Minimize intake of processed flour and high glycemic index sugar sources. Always choice whole grains instead of refined grains.
5. Eat lean animal protein and more plant-based sources of protein.
6. Add spices to your diet. Many of them are anti-inflammatory.

What can you Eat on the Anti-Inflammatory Diet?

With all of the different diet types out there, from gluten-free to alkaline, it can be tough to keep track of what's okay and what isn't. While the ins and outs of the gluten-free diet have become relatively mainstream, other diets, like the anti-inflammatory diet, have had their moment in the public spotlight. It's said that the anti-inflammatory diet can help combat issues such as digestion problems, fatigue, moodiness, issues with weight management, and food cravings. Inflammation also happens to be seen as the root cause of many diseases, like arthritis, diabetes, and cancer. However, you should always consult a professional when dealing with any of these problems, but one of the ways that we can help ourselves is by introducing more anti-inflammatory foods into our diet.

So, what can you eat on an anti-inflammatory diet? Dark, leafy greens like spinach and kale, broccoli, sweet potato, legumes like lentils and cooked beans, cauliflower, and soy-based products like tofu and tempeh all have the green light. You're not limited in the types of fruits you can consume, but anti-oxidant rich ones like blueberries and cherries are at the top of the list. Whole grains, especially sprouted whole grains, and whole grains-based pastas and breads are also great — the key to enjoying bread and pasta on an anti-inflammatory diet is to avoid processed wheat flours. Last, but not least, are green tea, garlic, and turmeric, which are easy to include in your everyday diet.

The beauty of the anti-inflammatory diet is that recommended foods are typically simple to buy and prepare. The anti-inflammatory diet includes foods high in omega-3 fatty acids, antioxidants, fiber, and spices. It also promotes a balance of omega-3 and omega-6 fatty acids. "Most people consume an excess of omega-6 fatty acids, from which the body synthesizes hormones that promote inflammation. These omega-6 polyunsaturated fats are found in vegetable oils, seeds, and nuts, and are used in many snack foods and fast foods. On the other hand, omega-3 fatty acids have an anti-inflammatory effect. They are found in foods including oily fish, walnuts, flax and hemp seeds, and to a lesser degree, in soy and canola oils and sea vegetables. Based on a 2,000-calorie-a-day diet, you are expected to consume 160 to 200 grams of carbohydrates, between 80 and 120 grams of protein, 40 grams of fiber, and around 67 grams of fat, with a ratio of 1:2:1 of saturated to monounsaturated to polyunsaturated.

The anti-inflammatory diet doesn't prescribe a specific eating routine. Instead, it just recommends that you eat four to six times each day, and try to include carbohydrates, protein, and fat with every meal or snack.

Rules For Optimal Health

If you want to eat for long-term health, lowering inflammation is crucial. Inflammation in the body causes or contributes to many debilitating, chronic illnesses—including osteoarthritis, rheumatoid arthritis, heart disease, Alzheimer's disease, Parkinson's disease, and even cancer. Although the goal is to optimize health, many people find they also lose weight by following an anti-inflammatory eating pattern. In general, follow these rules for optimal health:

Consume at Least 25 Grams of Fiber Every Day

A fiber-rich diet helps reduce inflammation by supplying naturally occurring anti-inflammatory phytonutrients found in fruits, vegetables, and other whole foods. To get your fill of fiber, seek out whole grains, fruits, and vegetables. The best sources include whole grains such as barley and oatmeal; vegetables like okra, eggplant, and onions; and a variety of fruits like bananas (3 grams of fiber per banana) and blueberries (3.5 grams of fiber per cup).

Eat a Minimum of Nine Servings of Fruits And Vegetables Every Day

9 cups raw or 4½ cups cooked

One "serving" is half a cup of a cooked fruit or vegetable, or one cup of a raw leafy vegetable. For an extra punch, add anti-inflammatory herbs and spices — such as turmeric and ginger — to your cooked fruits and vegetables to increase their antioxidant capacity.

Eat Four Servings of Both Alliums and Crucifers Every Week

Alliums include garlic, scallions, onions, and leek, while crucifers refer to vegetables such as broccoli, cabbage, cauliflower, mustard greens, and Brussels sprouts. Because of their powerful antioxidant properties, consuming a weekly average of four servings of each can help lower your risk of cancer. If you like the taste, I recommend eating a clove of garlic a day!

Limit Saturated Fat to 10 Percent of Your Daily Calories

By keeping saturated fat low (that's about 20 grams per 2,000 calories), you'll help reduce the risk of heart disease. You should also limit red meat to once per week and marinate it with herbs, spices, and tart, unsweetened fruit juices to reduce the toxic compounds formed during cooking.

Consume Foods Rich In Omega-3 Fatty Acids

Research shows that omega-3 fatty acids reduce inflammation and may help lower risk of chronic diseases such as heart disease, cancer, and arthritis — conditions that often have a high inflammatory process at their root. Aim to eat lots of foods high in omega-3 fatty acids like flax meal, walnuts, and beans such as navy, kidney and soy. It is also recommended you take a good-quality omega-3 supplement. And of course, consume cold-water fish such as salmon, oysters, herring, mackerel, trout, sardines, and anchovies. Speaking of which:

Eat Fish at Least Three Times a Week

Choose both low-fat fish such as sole and flounder, and cold-water fish that contain healthy fats, like the ones mentioned above.

Use Oils That Contain Healthy Fats

The body requires fat, but choose the fats that provide you with benefits. Virgin and extra-virgin olive oil (organic if possible like this one) and expeller-pressed canola are the best bets for anti-inflammatory benefits. Other options include high-oleic, expeller-pressed versions of sunflower and safflower oil.

Eat Healthy Snacks at Least Once a Day

If you're a snacker, aim for fruit, plain or unsweetened Greek-style yogurt (it contains more protein per serving), celery sticks, carrots, or nuts like pistachios, almonds, and walnuts.

Avoid Processed Foods and Refined Sugars

NO

This includes any food that contains high-fructose corn syrup or is high in sodium, which contribute to inflammation throughout the body. Avoid refined sugars whenever possible and artificial sweeteners altogether. The dangers of excess fructose have been widely cited and include increased insulin resistance (which can lead to type-2 diabetes), raised uric acid levels, raised blood pressure, increased risk of fatty liver disease, and more.

Cut Out Trans Fats

In 2006, the FDA required food manufacturers to identify trans fats on nutrition labels, and for good reason — studies show that people who eat foods high in trans fats have higher levels of C-reactive protein, a biomarker for inflammation in the body. A good rule of thumb is to always read labels and steer clear of products that contain the words "hydrogenated" or "partially hydrogenated oils." Vegetable shortenings, select margarines, crackers, and cookies are just a few examples of foods that might contain trans fats.

Sweeten Meals With Phytonutrient-Rich Fruits, And Flavor Foods With Spices

Most fruits and vegetables are loaded with important phytonutrients. In order to naturally sweeten your meals, try adding apples, apricots, berries, and even carrots. And for flavoring savory meals, go for spices that are known for their anti-inflammatory properties, including cloves, cinnamon, turmeric, rosemary, ginger, sage, and thyme.

？

Foods to Avoid on Anti-Inflammatory Diet

Studies show that foods high in saturated fat and sugar and low in fiber trigger inflammation. These include the highly processed or packaged "junk" foods you typically find in the middle aisles of the grocery store. Foods that cause inflammation and should be avoided include processed meats, fried foods, soda, lard, full-fat dairy products, partially hydrogenated oils, foods with a long shelf life (cakes, cookies, crackers, etc.), foods high in simple carbohydrates and refined grains, and any foods that trigger intolerance reactions. Here are some examples of food you need to avoid

- Microwaveable meals
- Easy macaroni and cheese
- Fast food
- Frozen pizza
- Fried foods (French fries, fish sticks, onion rings, fried mozzarella sticks)
- White bread or anything else made with white flour like cake, donuts, cookies and pastries
- Red meat
- Candy
- Chips

- Soda (even diet!) and energy drinks
- Sugary snack foods and cereals

If you're not sure something is good or bad to eat, check the grocery list below. Stay away from anything made with:

- Partially hydrogenated oils or trans fats
- High fructose corn syrup
- Food coloring
- Ingredients you don't know

And beware of packaged foods that seem "healthy." Just because something says it is "natural," "organic" or "made with real fruit" doesn't mean it's not highly processed and loaded with sugar. All this doesn't mean having the occasional soda or cupcake is totally off-limits. But in general, try not to eat these types of foods more than once a week.

?

Choosing Good Fats for an Anti-Inflammation Diet

Consuming fat in an anti-inflammatory diet isn't forbidden but the key is knowing which fats are good, which are bad, and which aren't too awful in moderation. "Fat" has become a dirty word in the dietary world, but some fats are not only good for you but necessary for a healthy lifestyle:

Good Fats

Polyunsaturated and monounsaturated fats are essential to keeping the good fat in your body in check. Good sources of these fats include olive oil, nuts (almonds, pecans, peanuts, and walnuts, for example), oatmeal, sesame oil and seeds, and soybeans, as well as the omega-3 fatty acids found in salmon, herring, trout, and sardines. The total fat intake for a day should equal between 20 and 35 percent of total calories for the day, and just 10 percent of those calories should be made up of the "bad" fats.

Not-So-Good Fats

Some foods with saturated fats are okay in moderation, as long as your "moderation" doesn't mean daily. Splurge every now and then, but remember that each splurge takes away from the good you're doing for your body. Sources of saturated fats include fatty meats, butter, cheese, ice cream, and palm oil. Not all saturated fats are bad: Coconut and coconut oil, while considered saturated fats, are actually healthy and beneficial to an anti-inflammatory diet.

Awful Fats

Avoid trans fats at all costs. Trans fats are the bad fats found in cakes, pastries, margarine, and shortening, among other foods. One quick and easy way to identify trans fats is to consider the form: Is the fat a solid that can melt and then solidify again? If so, chances are it's a trans fat. Reading the labels on foods is another way to identify trans fats: Hydrogenated or partially hydrogenated fats are trans fats, too.

Anti-Inflammatory Diet
Grocery List

VEGETABLES

- Radish
- Jalapeno or Thai Red Pepper *No*
- Thin Asparagus
- Arugula Leaves
- Seedless Cucumber
- Leafy Greens
- Green Onions
- Avocado
- Zucchini
- Red Cabbage
- Vegetable Platter: Carrot, Grape *NO* Potatoes, Celery, Broccoli

DIARY

No ~~Plain Yoghurt~~
- Almond Milk or Coconut Milk
- Eggs
- Ghee or Clarified Butter
No ~~Buffalo Styled Mozzarella~~

BAKING SUPPLIES

- Raw Honey

- Coconut Sugar

- Coconut Flour

- Baking Powder

- Maple Syrup

- Tapioca Starch

- Arrowroot Starch

- Vanilla Extract

- Vanilla Protein Powder or Collagen Powder

- Chickpea Flour

- Nutritional Yeast

FRUIT

- Oranges

- Large Bananas

- Apples

- Berries

- Lemon and Limes

- Watermelon

- Date and Raisins

- Pineapples

- HERBS

- Basil
- Mint Leaves
- Cilantro
- Ginger Knob
- Fresh Oregano Leaves
- Garlic
- Rosemary

NUT AND SEEDS

- Sesame Seeds
- Ground Flaxseed
- Chia Seed
- Pumpkin Seed
- Silvered Almond
- Raw Cashew
- Crushed Salted Nuts
- PANTRY STAPLES
- Onion Powder
- Ground Cumin
- Paprika
 Sea Salt
 Black Pepper
 Ground Cinnamon
- Garlic Powder

- Anise Seed
- Turmeric
- Tamari Source
- Chia Tea Bags
- ~~Chili Sauce~~
- Rice Vinegar
- Extra Virgin Oil
- Coconut Oil
- Sesame Oil
- Avocado Oil
- Dried Parsley *fresh*
- Ground Mustard
- Apple Cider Vinegar
- Chicken Broth — *No Salt*
- Unsweetened Coconut Flakes
- Dijon Mustard
- ~~Fish Sauce~~
- Paleo Mayonnaise
- Almond Butter
- Sunflower Seed Butter
- Pesto
- Gluten Free or Paleo Tortillas

MEAT AND SEAFOODS

- Lean Beef
- Tilapia or Haddock

~~ Roasted Chicken

- Sockeye Salmon

GRAINS

- Quinoa
- Gluten Free Rolled Oats
- Jasmine Rice

Making Anti-Inflammatory Food Choices

After you discover the link between inflammation and chronic illness and the important role food has in fighting them both, you need an idea of what foods will help you treat and even prevent inflammation. Here are some ideas to guide your food choices for different meals:

Breakfasts

Turn to natural ingredients in homemade smoothies, such as berries, honey, and Greek or non-dairy yogurt. Some egg dishes, particularly those made with organic eggs, can help lower inflammation as well. Want toast? Try something gluten- and wheat-free, like rice breads.

Snacks and Appetizers

The easiest natural snack is a handful of fruit or fresh veggies. Grab a good crispy apple or a handful of snow peas and you've done your body proud. Want to make it a little snappier? Throw together an avocado dip, stuff an oversized portobello mushroom with kale and other heart-healthy ingredients, or grab a handful of dates. Fruits and nuts are great on-the-go snacks and are filled with vitamins and nutrients, as well as the benefits of omega-3 fatty acids found in most nuts.

Soups and Salads

Sometimes there's nothing better than a good cup of soup or a nice salad, but it's easy to get fooled by those that may not be as healthy as they appear. Good soups for fighting inflammation include vegetable soup with a butternut squash base or miso soup with gluten-free noodles. Many people have inflammatory reactions to tomatoes and other nightshade fruits and vegetables, so it's a good idea to stay away from tomato-based soups with potatoes and bell peppers. For salads, steer toward the darker greens and fresh organic toppers, dressed with just a sprinkling of vinegar or olive oil.

ouch

Main Dishes

Some good anti-inflammatory options for main dishes include most kinds of fish, which is full of omega-3 fatty acids. If you're looking for a bit of protein in your main dish, turn to chicken or even tofu. Try to avoid red meat if possible, but use grass-fed meat if you must go that route.

Dessert

Think "desserts" and the word "sweet" is likely the first to pop into mind — and just because you're trying to fight inflammation doesn't mean you have to fight your sweet tooth, too. Try some chopped fruit and melted dark chocolate to get the vitamins in the fruit and the rich antioxidants in dark chocolate. Need something creamy? Try adding some vanilla extract or honey to a Greek or non-dairy yogurt or, if dairy isn't a problem for you, add it to a little bit of light ricotta cheese.

?

Changing Your Cooking Methods to Reduce Inflammation

An anti-inflammatory diet begins with choosing the right foods, but it continues with using anti-inflammatory cooking methods to prepare those foods. You can undo a lot of the good in your healthy foods by cooking them the wrong way. Here are some tips on getting the most out of your cooking methods:

Baking

Put your food in the center of a glass or ceramic baking dish, leaving room around the sides to let hot air circulate. Setting veggies on the bottom of a dish, under meat or fish, adds moisture and enhances flavor. Cover the dish to let the food cook with steam while retaining its natural juices.

Steaming

Use a vegetable steamer, rice cooker, or bamboo steamer — or create your own steamer with a covered pot and slotted insert — to gently cook a variety of foods. Take care not to overcook vegetables, fish, or seafood. Marinate foods with herbs such as rosemary and sage before steaming, and add spices such as ginger and turmeric to foods while steaming to infuse the flavor into the food.

Poaching

This gentle cooking method requires no additional fats, such as oil. Bring poaching liquid (water or stock, usually) to a boil and add your meat, seafood, or veggies; reduce the heat and simmer until done for a lowfat, flavorful result. Save the poaching liquid from meat or fish and use it as the base of a soup.

Stir-Frying

This method allows you to cook with a small amount of oil (or none at all) at high temperatures for a very short amount of time so that the food absorbs very little oil. Vegetables in particular retain their beneficial nutrients.

Grilling and Broiling

Reserve grilling for fish and veggies, which don't need much cooking time. Grilling and broiling meats involves excessive temperatures that cause the fats and proteins in meat and protein turn into heterocyclic amines (HAs), which may raise the risk of certain cancers.

Microwaving

As for giving your food a 🄯uick zap in the microwave, that convenience appliance destroys the nutrients in food because of the high heat, so you should avoid this cooking method.

🄯

Benefits of the Anti-Inflammatory Diet

The anti-inflammatory diet is a fiber and nutrient-rich eating pattern that focuses on whole foods and reduces or eliminates foods known to contribute to chronic inflammation. Potential benefits of the diet include maintenance of health and wellness and prevention of chronic diseases associated with inflammation, such as type 2 diabetes, heart disease and some forms of cancer. Here are some of the benefits of anti-inflammatory diet:

Reduces Inflammation

All of the foods on the anti-inflammatory diet have been shown to help with chronic inflammation and disease risk in some way. Each of the recommended food groups has a substance, such as resveratrol and antioxidants, that helps reduce inflammation.

Promotes Healthy Eating

Each food on the anti-inflammatory diet contains vitamins, minerals, and other essential nutrients. Overall, the diet promotes a good balance between carbohydrates, fats, and proteins and encourages you to include colorful produce, especially berries, tomatoes, orange and yellow fruits, cruciferous veggies, and dark leafy greens.

Not Restrictive

The anti-inflammatory diet is very easy to follow. There are no strict meal plans, and you're free to modify the diet to best suit your needs, as long as you stick to the anti-inflammatory food pyramid. You can be creative with meals on the anti-inflammatory diet because it includes so many food groups. Eating out and drinking alcohol are also permitted on the anti-inflammatory diet, which makes it much more conducive to the typical lifestyle.

The abundance of Recipes: Since the anti-inflammatory diet is so popular, thousands of compliant recipes already exist. There is no need to start from scratch!

Overall, the anti-inflammatory diet promotes a healthy eating pattern that will ensure you consume adequate levels of all of the macronutrients, micronutrients, fiber, and antioxidants.

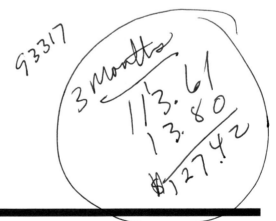

30-Day Anti-Inflammatory Meal Plan

Food plays an important role in controlling inflammation. We've put together 4 full week of recipes using foods that are known for their anti-inflammatory properties. Help manage your rheumatoid arthritis (RA) by eating right. Because inflammation can be caused by plenty of other factors besides food, like low activity levels, stress and lack of sleep, incorporating healthy lifestyle habits into your daily routine can also help prevent inflammation. To get the most anti-inflammatory benefits, pair this healthy meal plan with regular physical activity, stress-relieving practices, and a good night's sleep every night at least 7 hours per night. Whether you're working to actively decrease inflammation or are simply looking for a wholesome eating plan, this 30-day anti-inflammatory meal plan alongside the 7-day physical activities can help. These anti-inflammatory recipes include delicious and healthy options for:

- Breakfast
- Lunch
- Dinner
- Drinks
- Snacks/Dessert

In this 2000-calorie everyday healthy meal plan, here is the anti-inflammatory diet meal plans for 4 weeks of delicious, wholesome meals and snacks, plus meal preparation tips to set you up for a successful week ahead.

30-DAY MEAL PLAN AT A GLANCE

	BREAKFAST	LUNCH	SNACKS	DINNER
		WEEK 1		
DAY 1	Gingerbread Oatmeal	Kale Caesar Salad with Grilled Chicken Wrap	Chia Seed Pudding	Baked Tilapia with Pecan Rosemary Topping
DAY 2	Oat Porridge with Berries	Grilled Sauerkraut, Hummus, and Avocado Sandwich	Power Balls	Salmon Cakes
DAY 3	Kale Pineapple smoothie	Quinoa and Citrus Salad	Matcha Smoothie Bowl	Root Vegetable Tagine
DAY 4	Turmeric Oatmeal	Sweet Potato And Chickpea Stew	Citrus Salad with Greek Yogurt	Salmon with Greens and Cauliflower Rice
DAY 5	Coconut Flour Pancakes	Coconut Rice and Watermelon Salad Bowls	Trail Mix	Curry Shrimp and Vegetable
DA	Oat Porridge	Lettuce Wraps with Smoked	Citrus Salad with	Broiled Salmon

Y 6	with Berries	Trout	Tarragon	with Spinach
DAY 7	Smoked Salmon, Avocado, and Poached Eggs on Toast	Rosemary Citrus One Pan Baked Salmon	Maple Sesame Quinoa Bars (Nut Free)	Lentil and Chicken Soup with Sweet Potato

WEEK 2

DAY 8	Buckwheat and Chia Seed Porridge	Cauliflower Steak with Beans and Tomatoes	Citrus Salad with Greek Yogurt	Vegetarian Chili
DAY 9	Turmeric Oatmeal	Pickled Pineapple Baja Fish Tacos	Trail Mix	Asian Zoodle Flu Buster Soup
DAY 10	Red Velvet Smoothie	Apple Kimchi Salad with Beef	Power Balls	Roasted Cauliflower, Fennel, And Ginger Soup
DAY 11	Golden Milk	Lentil, Beetroot, And Hazelnut Salad	Chia Seed Pudding	Sesame Shrimp Stir Fry
DAY	Chai Spiced Chia Smoothie	Cooked Spinach and	No Bake Lemon	

12	Bowls	Pine Nuts	Coconut Paleo Energy Bars	
DAY 13	Cherry Coconut Porridge	Cranberry Walnut Salad	Chia Seed Pudding	Curried Potatoes with Poached Eggs
DAY 14	Yogurt Parfaits with Raspberries and Chia Seeds	Detox Broccoli Salad without Mayo	Rosemary-Tangerine Cooler	Moroccan Red Lentil Soup with Chard

WEEK 3

DAY 15	Raspberry Smoothie	Quinoa and Citrus Salad	Apple Chips	Slow Cooker Turkey Chili
DAY 16	Rhubarb, Apple, and Ginger Muffins	Rosemary Citrus One Pan Baked Salmon	Raw Veggies with Homemade Vegan Ranch Dressing	Italian-Style Stuffed Red Peppers
DAY 17	Strawberry Veggie Smoothie	Kale Caesar Salad with Grilled Chicken Wrap	Lemon Turmeric Energy Balls	Cooked Spinach and Pine Nuts
DAY	Green Tea Latte	Red Quinoa	Chia Seed	Baked Tilapia

18	Overnight Oats	Salad	Pudding	with Pecan Rosemary Topping
DAY 19	Pecan Banana Bread Overnight Oats	Salmon with Greens and Cauliflower Rice	Coconut Lemon Bars	Chinese Chicken Salad
DAY 20	Turmeric Latte	Broiled Salmon with Spinach	Coconut Lemon Bars	Instant Pot Sweet Potato Curry Stew
DAY 21	Turmeric Oatmeal	Zucchini Noodles with Roasted Halibut	Citrus Vinaigrette	Salmon and Quinoa Bowls with Kale and Tahini-Yogurt Sauce
WEEK 4			
DAY 22	Cinnamon Spice Roasted Pepitas	Strawberry Chia Jam	Sweet Potato Toast with Blueberries	Spiced Lentil Soup
DAY	Cherry Coconut	Zucchini Noodles with	Power Balls	Polenta with

23	Porridge	Roasted Halibut		Wild Mushroom Bolognese
DAY 24	Oat porridge with Berries	Dukkah Roasted Vegetables Salad	Matcha Smoothie Bowl	Slow Cooker Turkey Chili
DAY 25	Coffee and Mint Parfait	Cranberry Walnut Salad	Sweet Potato Toast with Blueberries	Curried Potatoes with Poached Eggs
DAY 26	Turmeric Oatmeal	Lettuce Wraps with Smoked Trout	Coconut Lemon Bars	Salmon with Greens and Cauliflower Rice
DAY 27	Golden Milk	Thai Pumpkin Soup	Lemon Turmeric Energy Balls	One Pan Lemon Sage Baked Chicken and Olives
DAY 28	5-Minute Herb Baked Eggs	Tomato Basil Garlic Chicken	Citrus Vinaigrette	Baked Turkey Meatballs
DA	Ancient Grains	Kale Caesar	Rosemary-	Crockpo

Y 29	Breakfast Bowl	Salad with Grilled Chicken Wrap	Tangerine Cooler	t Bean Bologne se
DA Y 30	Coconut Flour Pancakes	Quinoa and Citrus Salad	Apple Chips	One-Pan Roasted Chicken with Turmeri c

DAY 1

?

BREAKFAST

Gingerbread Oatmeal

Start to End: 35 minutes

Servings: 4

Ingredients

- 4 cups water
- 1 cup steel cut oats
- 1 1/2 tbsp. ground cinnamon
- 1/4 tsp. ground coriander
- 1/4 tsp. ground cloves
- 1/4 tsp. ground ginger
- 1/4 tsp. ground allspice
- 1/8 tsp. ground nutmeg
- 1/4 tsp. ground cardamom

- maple syrup to taste

How to Make

1. Cook the oats to package directions but include the spices when you add the oats to the water.
2. When finished cooking, add maple syrup to taste.

LUNCH

Kale Caesar Salad with Grilled Chicken Wrap

Start to End: 10 minutes

Servings: 2

- Ingredients
- 8 ounces grilled chicken, thinly sliced
- 6 cups curly kale, cut into bite sized pieces
- 1 cup cherry tomatoes, quartered
- 3/4 cup finely shredded Parmesan cheese
- ½ coddled egg (cooked about 1 minute)
- 1 clove garlic, minced
- 1/2 tsp Dijon mustard
- 1 teaspoon honey or agave

- 1/8 cup fresh lemon juice
- 1/8 cup olive oil
- Kosher salt and freshly ground black pepper
- 2 Lavash flat breads or two large tortillas

How to Make

1 In a bowl, mix together the half of a coddled egg, minced garlic, mustard, honey, lemon juice and olive oil. Whisk until you have formed a dressing. Season to taste with salt and pepper.

2 Add the kale, chicken and cherry tomatoes and toss to coat with the dressing and ¼ cup of the shredded parmesan.

3 Spread out the two lavash flatbreads. Evenly distribute the salad over the two wraps and sprinkle each with ¼ cup of parmesan.

4 Roll up the wraps and slice in half. Eat immediately

?

SNACK

Chia Seed Pudding

Start to End: 10 minutes

Servings: 1

Ingredients

- One 13.5-ounce can light coconut milk
- 3 tablespoons chia seeds
- 3 tablespoons pure maple syrup
- 1/2 cup fresh pineapple chunks
- 2 medium kiwis, peeled and sliced
- 1/4 cup raspberries
- 2 tablespoons roasted almonds, chopped

How to Make

1. Special equipment: four 8-ounce glass jars with lids.

2. Stir together the coconut milk, chia seeds and maple syrup in a medium bowl.
3. Divide the mixture evenly among four 8-ounce glass jars.
4. Screw on the lids, and refrigerate overnight, covered, to allow the seeds to plump and the mixture to thicken into a loose pudding.
5. Arrange the pineapples, kiwis, raspberries and almonds in separate layers on top of the pudding.
6. Cover with the lid, and keep refrigerated for up to 1 day.⏷

DINNER

Baked Tilapia with Pecan Rosemary Topping

Start to End: 35 minutes

Servings: 4

Ingredients

- 1/3 cup chopped raw pecans
- 1/3 cup whole wheat panko breadcrumbs
- 2 tsps chopped fresh rosemary
- ½ tsp coconut palm sugar or brown sugar
- 1/8 tsp salt
- 1 pinch cayenne pepper
- 1 ½ tsp olive oil
- 1 egg white

- 4 ounces each tilapia fillets

How to Make

1. Preheat oven to 350 degrees F.
2. In a small baking dish, stir together pecans, breadcrumbs, rosemary, coconut palm sugar, salt and cayenne pepper.
3. Add the olive oil and toss to coat the pecan mixture.
4. Bake until the pecan mixture is light golden brown, 7 to 8 minutes.
5. Increase the heat to 400 degrees F. Coat a large glass baking dish with cooking spray.
6. In a shallow dish, whisk the egg white. Working with one tilapia at a time, dip the fish in the egg white and then the pecan mixture, lightly coating each side.
7. Place the fillets in the prepared baking dish.
8. Press the remaining pecan mixture into the top of the tilapia fillets.
9. Bake until the tilapia is just cooked through, about 10 minutes. Serve. ⏹

DAY 2

?

BREAKFAST

Oat Porridge with Berries

Start to End: 30 minutes

Servings: 4

Ingredients

For The Oats:

- 1 cup steel cut oats
- 3 cups water
- pinch of salt

Toppings:

- fresh or frozen fruit/berries
- a handful of sliced almonds, pepitas, hemp seeds, or other nut/seed

- unsweetened kefir, homemade
- drizzle of maple syrup, sprinkling of coconut sugar, a few drops of stevia, or any other sweetener

How to Make

1. Add the oats to a small saucepan and place over medium-high heat. Allow to toast, stirring or shaking the pan fre🄯uently, for 2-3 minutes.
2. Add the water and bring to a boil. Reduce the heat to a simmer, and let cook for about 25 minutes, or until the oats are tender enough for your liking. (The oats will thicken up as they cool -- if you prefer them a bit more porridge, add a splash more water, or some milk or dairy-free alternative.)
3. Serve with berries, nuts/seeds (or a handful of granola), a splash of kefir, and any sweetener you like, to taste. 🄯

LUNCH

Grilled Sauerkraut, Hummus, and Avocado Sandwich

Start to End: 25 minutes

Servings: 4

Ingredients

- 8 slices pumpernickel bread
- vegan buttery spread (or regular butter)
- 1 cup hummus (roasted garlic flavor, divided)
- 1 cup sauerkraut
- 1 avocado

How to Make

1. Preheat oven to 450 degrees F (230 degrees C).

2. Spread butter on one side of each of the 8 slices of bread, and place 4 of the butter side down on a baking sheet.
3. Take about half of the hummus and distribute over the 4 slices of bread.
4. Distribute the sauerkraut over the hummus on each slice.
5. Distribute the avocado slices over the sauerkraut.
6. For the remaining 4 slices of bread, spread hummus on the side without butter and place hummus side down on the avocado slices.
7. Bake in the oven for 6-8 minutes, then flip the sandwiches and bake about 6 minutes more, until the sandwiches are golden brown and crispy. (Alternatively, you can grill them on the stove top on a griddle or in a skillet).

SNACK

Power Balls

Start to End: 45 minutes

Servings: 25

Ingredients

- ½ Cup puffed millet
- 1 cup puffed kamut or puffed rice
- ½ cup diced dried plums
- 1/3 cup semisweet chocolate chips
- ¼ cup sesame seeds
- 1/3 cup sunflower butter, at room temperature
- ½ cup honey
- ¾ cup shredded unsweetened coconut

How to Make

1. In a large bowl, toss together the puffed millet and puffed kamut or rice.
2. Add the dried plums, chocolate chips, and sesame seeds.
3. Stir in the sunflower butter and the honey. You should have a nice sticky mess!
4. Cover the bowl with plastic wrap and refrigerate for 30 minutes.
5. Place the coconut in a small bowl. Using a tablespoon, scoop the mixture and form it into 1-inch (2.5cm) balls with your hands.
6. Roll the balls in the coconut and transfer to a container.
7. You can store the power balls in the refrigerator for up to 1 week, or in the freezer in a zip-top freezer bag for up to 1 month, but I bet they won't last that long!

?

DINNER

Salmon Cakes

Start to End: 2 hours 20 minutes

Servings: 5

Ingredients

- ½ pound fresh salmon
- Good olive oil
- Kosher salt and freshly ground black pepper
- 4 tablespoons unsalted butter
- ¾ cup small-diced red onion
- 1 ½ cups small-diced celery
- ½ cup small-diced red bell pepper
- ½ cup small-diced yellow bell pepper
- ¼ cup minced fresh flat-leaf parsley
- 1 tbsp capers, drained
- ¼ tsp hot sauce (recommended: Tabasco)

- ½ tsp Worcestershire sauce
- 1 ½ tsps crab boil seasoning (recommended: Old Bay)
- 3 slices stale bread, crusts removed
- ½ cup good mayonnaise
- 2 tsps Dijon mustard
- 2 extra-large eggs, lightly beaten

How to Make

1. Preheat the oven to 350 degrees F.
2. Place the salmon on a sheet pan, skin side down. Brush with olive oil and sprinkle with salt and pepper.
3. Roast for 15 to 20 minutes, until just cooked. Remove from the oven and cover tightly with aluminum foil. Allow to rest for 10 minutes and refrigerate until cold.
4. Meanwhile, place 2 tablespoons of the butter, 2 tablespoons olive oil, the onion, celery, red and yellow bell peppers, parsley, capers, hot sauce, Worcestershire sauce, crab boil seasoning, 1/2 teaspoon salt, and 1/2 teaspoon pepper in a large saute pan over medium-low heat and cook until the vegetables are soft, approximately 15 to 20 minutes. Cool to room temperature.
5. Break the bread slices in pieces and process the bread in a food processor fitted with a steel blade. You should have about 1 cup of bread crumbs. Place the bread crumbs on a sheet pan and toast in the oven for 5 minutes until lightly browned, tossing occasionally.
6. Flake the chilled salmon into a large bowl. Add the bread crumbs, mayonnaise, mustard, and eggs. Add the vegetable mixture and mix well. Cover and chill in the refrigerator for 30 minutes. Shape into 10 (2 1/2 to 3-ounce) cakes.

7. Heat the remaining 2 tablespoons butter and 2 tablespoons olive oil in a large saute pan over medium heat. In batches, add the salmon cakes and fry for 3 to 4 minutes on each side, until browned. Drain on paper towels; keep them warm in a preheated 250 degree F oven and serve hot.

⁇

DAY 3

BREAKFAST

Kale Pineapple Smoothie

Start to End: 5 minutes

Servings: 2

Ingredients

- 2 cups lightly packed chopped kale leaves
- ¾ cup unsweetened vanilla almond milk
- 1 frozen medium banana — cut into chunks
- ¼ cup plain non-fat Greek yogurt
- ¼ cup frozen pineapple pieces
- 2 tablespoons peanut butter
- 1 to 3 teaspoons honey

How to Make

1. Place all ingredients in a blender in the order listed. Blend until smooth. Add more milk as needed to reach desired consistency.

LUNCH

Quinoa and Citrus Salad

Start to End: 10 minutes

Servings: 1

Ingredients

- 1 cup cooked quinoa, cooled
- 2 small oranges, supremed
- 1 celery rib, finely chopped
- 20g Brazil nuts, chopped
- 1 green onion, sliced
- ¼ cup fresh parsley, finely chopped

For the Dressing:

- juice from above oranges
- ½ tsp lemon juice
- ½ tsp fresh ginger, grated
- 1 tsp white wine vinegar
- 1 small clove garlic, minced
- ½ tsp salt
- ¼ tsp black pepper
- pinch cinnamon

How to Make

1. Cut the oranges into supremes, working over a bowl, in order not lose any of the juice.
2. When you've got all your supremes done, make sure to squeeze all the juice out of the "membranes" that are left behind.
3. Transfer that juice to your mini blender or food processor.
4. Add the rest of the ingredients for the dressing and blend until smooth.
5. Cut your orange supremes into bite size pieces and add them to a medium size mixing bowl. Add the rest of the ingredients, including the dressing, and stir until well combined.
6. Serve immediately, or keep in the refrigerator until ready to serve.

SNACK

Matcha Smoothie Bowl

Start to End: 5 minutes

Servings: 2

Ingredients

Smoothie:

- 2 peeled, sliced and frozen ripe bananas
- ¼ cup chopped ripe pineapple
- ¾ - 1 cup light coconut milk
- 2 tsp matcha green tea powder
- 1 heaping cup organic spinach or kale

Toppings (optional):

- Fresh berries
- Coconut flake

- Banana slices
- Chia Seeds
- Slivered roasted almonds

How to Make

1. Add frozen banana slices, pineapple (optional), lesser amount of coconut milk, matcha powder, and spinach to a blender and blend on high until creamy and smooth.
2. Add only as much coconut milk as you need to help it blend.
3. Taste and adjust flavor as needed, adding more banana (or a touch of maple syrup or stevia) for sweetness, matcha for more intense green tea flavor, or coconut milk for creaminess. Pineapple will add a little tart/tang, so add more if desired.
4. Divide between two serving bowls and top with desired toppings (optional). Bananas would make a delicious garnish as well.
5. Best when fresh, though leftovers keep well sealed in the refrigerator up to 24 hours. ⏺

DINNER

Root Vegetable Tagine

Start to End: 45 mins

Servings: 6

Ingredients

- 2 tbsps olive or coconut oil
- 1 large sweet onion diced
- 1 medium parsnip peeled and diced
- 2 large cloves garlic minced
- 1 tsp ground cumin
- ½ tsp ground ginger
- ½ tsp ground cinnamon
- 1 tsp sea salt
- ¼ tsp cayenne pepper
- 3 tbsps tomato paste

- 2 medium sweet potatoes peeled and diced
- 2 medium purple potatoes or sub regular Yukon gold, peeled and diced
- 2 bunches baby carrots or sub 2 medium diced carrots, peeled
- 1 quart vegetable stock
- 2 cups roughly chopped kale leaves
- 2 tbsps lemon juice
- ¼ cup cilantro leaves roughly chopped
- Pepitas or toasted slivered almonds optional, for serving

How to Make

1. In a large stock pot or Dutch oven, heat the oil. Sauté the onion over medium-high heat until soft, 5 minutes.
2. Add the parsnip and cook until beginning to turn golden brown, 3 more minutes. Stir in the garlic, ground cumin, ginger, cinnamon, salt, cayenne, and tomato paste.
3. Cook until very fragrant, 2 minutes.
4. Fold in the sweet potatoes, purple potatoes, and carrots. Cover with vegetable stock and bring to a boil.
5. Reduce the heat to medium-low and simmer, uncovered, stirring occasionally, until the vegetables are tender, about 20 minutes.
6. Stir in the kale and lemon juice. Simmer for another 2 minutes, until the leaves are vibrant and slightly wilted.
7. Garnish with the cilantro and nuts, if using, and serve over quinoa or couscous.

DAY 4

⸮

BREAKFAST

Turmeric Oatmeal

Start to End: 20 minutes

Servings: 1

Ingredients

Oatmeal:

- ½ cup Whole Rolled Oats
- 1 cup Water
- 1 splash Oat Milk or any other plant milk you like
- ½ tsp Turmeric Powder

Toppings:

- Raspberries
- Blueberries

- Mixed Seeds
- Flaked Almonds
- Dried Cranberries
- Desiccated Coconut
- Mint Leaves
- Maple Syrup (optional)

How to Make

1. Measure the oats, hemp milk, water and spices into a saucepan.
2. Cook over a medium to high heat for about 5 minutes, until it reaches you desired consistency.
3. Top up with raspberries, blueberries, almonds, cranberries and whatever you fancy.

?

LUNCH

Sweet Potato And Chickpea Stew

Start to End: 1 hour 15 minutes

Servings: 6

Ingredients

- 2 tbsps olive oil
- 1 small white onion, chopped
- 2 carrots, chopped
- 2 garlic cloves, minced
- 1-inch piece of ginger, minced
- 1 tsp cumin
- 1 tsp paprika
- ¼ tsp ground turmeric
- Pinch of salt and pepper
- 1 cup vegetable stock

- 2 medium-size sweet potatoes, peeled and diced
- 2 14-ounce cans chickpeas
- 1 14-ounce can coconut milk

How to Make

1. Heat the olive oil in a large Dutch oven or pot, set over medium heat.
2. Add the onion and carrots to the pot and cook, stirring, until tender, approximately 8-10 minutes.
3. Add the garlic, ginger, and spices to the pot, and cook for an additional minute.
4. Add the remaining ingredients to the pot and bring to a boil. Once boiling, cover and reduce the heat to medium-low.
5. Simmer for approximately one hour, until the sweet potatoes are falling apart, and have started to "blend" into the stew.
6. Serve plain, or over rice with lime wedges and fresh mint, if desired.

?

SNACK

Citrus Salad with Greek Yogurt

Start to End: 20 minutes

Servings: 6

Ingredients

- 1 pink grapefruit, peeled
- 2 large tangerines or Minneolas, peeled
- 3 navel oranges
- ½ cup dried cranberries
- 2 tbsps honey
- ¼ tsp ground cinnamon
- 1 16- or 17.6-ounce container Greek yogurt
- 2/3 cup minced crystallized ginger

- ¼ cup golden brown sugar
- Additional dried cranberries

How to Make

1. Break grapefruit and tangerines into sections. Cut grapefruit sections into thirds; cut tangerine sections in half.
2. Transfer grapefruit, tangerines, and all juices to deep serving bowl.
3. Using small sharp knife, cut all peel and white pith from oranges. Slice oranges into 1/4-inch-thick rounds, then cut slices into quarters.
4. Add oranges and all juices to same bowl. Mix in 1/2 cup dried cranberries, honey, and cinnamon.
5. Cover and refrigerate at least 1 hour. Mix yogurt and ginger in bowl.
6. Spoon yogurt atop fruit. Sprinkle with brown sugar and dried cranberries.

?

DINNER

Salmon with Greens and Cauliflower Rice

Start to End: 1 hour

Servings: 2

Ingredients

- 2 salmon fillets, sustainably sourced or organic
- 10 to 12 Brussels sprouts, chopped in half
- 1 bunch kale, washed and shredded
- ½ head cauliflower, pulsed into cauliflower rice (you can use a whole cauliflower head if you wish)
- 3 tbsps olive or coconut oil
- 1 tsp curry powder
- Himalayan salt

For Marinade:

- ¼ cup tamari sauce

- 1 tsp Dijon mustard
- 1 tsp sesame oil
- 1 tsp honey or maple syrup (optional)
- 1 tbsp sesame seeds

How to Make

1. Preheat oven to 350°F.
2. Line a baking tray and add chopped Brussels sprouts. Coat with 1 tablespoon oil and season with salt. Add to oven and roast for 20 minutes.
3. Meanwhile, make marinade by combining all ingredients in a bowl and whisking until combined.
4. Remove Brussels sprouts after 20 minutes and add salmon fillets to the baking tray. Spoon marinade over salmon fillets and return to oven for a further 13 to 15 minutes, or until salmon is cooked to your liking.
5. While salmon is cooking, heat a pan over medium-high heat and add 1 tablespoon oil. Add kale and sauté until wilted (2 to 3 minutes). Remove from pan and set aside.
6. Heat remaining oil in pan and add cauliflower rice. Season with 1 teaspoon curry powder and salt and sauté until cooked (2 to 3 minutes).
7. Remove salmon and Brussels sprouts from oven and divide into two bowls. Add sautéed kale and cauliflower rice to bowls.

DAY 5

BREAKFAST

Coconut Flour Pancakes

Start to End: 20 minutes

Servings: 5

Ingredients

- 2 eggs and 1 extra egg white
- 1/3 cup of almond milk or coconut drinking milk
- 1/4 cup coconut flour -sifted
- 1 tbsp ground flaxseed
- 1 very ripe small banana or half a large banana
- 1 tsp vanilla extract
- 1 tsp ⊠uality apple cider vinegar or distilled vinegar
- ½ teaspoon baking powder
- 1/8 tsp salt
- 1/8 tsp cinnamon optional

- Optional sweetener of choice

How to Make

1. First place egg and milk in a blender or bowl to mix/beat. If you're making the banana version, blend the banana in with the eggs and milk first.
2. Mix in the the coconut flour (a little at a time, whisking) with the egg/milk mix until smooth and not clumpy.
3. Gently stir in the remaining ingredients and beat/blend again until smooth batter is formed. Place in fridge to set for 10-15 minutes.
4. Remove from fridge once batter has set.
5. Heat a skillet to medium high, adding a few teaspoons of oil to coat the pan.
6. Once hot, scoop 1/4 cup batter and pour into the center of the pan. Pancakes flip better with thinner batter (See notes). Also, a crepe pan or non stick griddle for pancakes works best!
7. Cook until the edges start to brown or the middle starts to bubble, which is usually no more than 2 -3 minutes.
8. Flip over and let pancake cook another 1-3 minutes. See notes for cooking times.
9. Remove pancake and place on plate. Repeat to get 3-6 pancakes. The banana sweetened coconut flour pancakes will produce more. All 5-6 inches wide.
10. Top pancakes with extra berries, nuts, and, butter, optional maple syrup.

?

LUNCH

Coconut Rice and Watermelon Salad Bowls

Start to End: 25 minutes

Servings: 2

Ingredients

- cup jasmine rice
- 1 cup chopped watermelon
- ½ cup coconut cream
- 1/3 cup raisins or dried blueberries
- ½ cup chopped basil or mint
- ¼ cup honey
- coconut oil

- Dash of salt

How to Make

1. First prepare your rice. Cook according to directions. Usually 1:2 ratio of rice to water.
2. Drain, stir in 1 tbsp coconut oil and a dash of salt. Let it cool in fridge.
3. While the rice is cooling, chopped your herbs and watermelon. Once rice is cooled, stir in the coconut cream and honey.
4. spoon rice into 2 -3 bowls and top with raisins, watermelon, herbs, and more honey/coconut cream. Enjoy

?

SNACK

Trail Mix

Start to End: 2 minutes

Servings: 3

Ingredients

- 1 cup almonds
- 1 cup brazil nuts
- ¼ cup pumpkin seeds
- Handful goji berries
- Small sprinkle of toasted coconut flakes
- 2 sun-dried organic pineapple slices

How to Make

1. Combine all the ingredients and store in an airtight container in the fridge.
2. Divide into handful size portions and enjoy as a ⬚uick meal or healthy snack.

⬚

DINNER

Curry Shrimp and Vegetable

Start to End: 25 minutes

Servings: 4

Ingredients

- 3 tbsps butter or coconut oil
- 1 onion sliced
- 1 cup coconut milk
- 1-3 tsp curry powder
- 1 lb shrimp tails removed
- 1 bag frozen cauliflower or other frozen veggies of choice

How to Make

1. Melt butter or oil in skillet and add sliced onion.
2. Saute onion until it is slightly soft.

3. Meanwhile, steam vegetables.
4. When onion is softened add coconut milk, curry seasoning, and other spices if desired.
5. Cook a couple minutes to incorporate flavors.
6. Add thawed shrimp and cook approximately 5 minutes or until shrimp are cooked
7. Serve with steamed veggies of choice topped with butter and salad with homemade dressing.

DAY 6

BREAKFAST

Oat Porridge with Berries

Start to End: 30 minutes

Servings: 4

Ingredients

For the Oats:

- 1 cup steel cut oats
- 3 cups water
- pinch of salt

Toppings:

- fresh or frozen fruit/berries
- a handful of sliced almonds, pepitas, hemp seeds, or other nut/seed

- unsweetened kefir, homemade or store-bought
- drizzle of maple syrup, sprinkling of coconut sugar, a few drops of stevia, or any other sweetener

How to Make

1. Add the oats to a small saucepan and place over medium-high heat. Allow to toast, stirring or shaking the pan fre?uently, for 2-3 minutes.
2. Add the water and bring to a boil. Reduce the heat to a simmer, and let cook for about 25 minutes, or until the oats are tender enough for your liking. (The oats will thicken up as they cool -- if you prefer them a bit more porridge, add a splash more water, or some milk or dairy-free alternative.)
3. Serve with berries, nuts/seeds (or a handful of granola), a splash of kefir, and any sweetener you like, to taste. ?

LUNCH

Lettuce Wraps with Smoked Trout

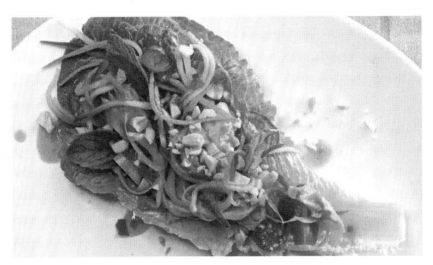

Start to End: 40 minutes

Servings: 4

Ingredients

- 2 medium carrots, peeled
- ½ unpeeled English hothouse cucumber (do not remove seeds)
- ¼ cup thinly sliced shallots
- ¼ cup thinly sliced jalapeño chiles with seeds (preferably red; about 2 large)
- 2 tbsps fresh lime juice or unseasoned rice vinegar
- 1 tbsp sugar
- 1 tbsp fish sauce

- 2 4.5-ounce packages skinless smoked trout fillets,** broken into bite-size pieces (about 2 cups)
- 1 cup diced grape tomatoes
- 1/2 cup whole fresh mint leaves
- 1/2 cup small whole fresh basil leaves
- 16 small to medium inner leaves of romaine lettuce (from about 2 hearts of romaine)
- 1/3 cup (about) Asian sweet chili sauce
- 1/4 cup finely chopped lightly salted dry-roasted peanuts

How to Make

1. Using vegetable peeler, shave carrots and cucumber lengthwise into ribbons. Cut ribbons into 3-inch-long sections, then cut sections into matchstick-size strips.
2. Place in large bowl. Add shallots, jalapeños, lime juice, sugar, and fish sauce; let marinate 30 minutes at room temperature.
3. Add trout pieces and tomatoes to vegetable mixture and toss to blend.
4. Transfer trout-vegetable mixture to large strainer and drain off liquid. Return trout-vegetable mixture to same bowl; add mint and basil and toss to blend.
5. Arrange lettuce leaves on large platter. Divide trout-vegetable salad among lettuce leaves. Drizzle sweet chili sauce over each salad and sprinkle with peanuts. ⏹

SNACK

Citrus Salad with Tarragon

Start to End: 25 minutes

Servings: 8

Ingredients

- ¼ cup sugar
- ¼ cup (packed) fresh tarragon leaves, plus more for serving
- 4 blood oranges
- 4 clementines
- 2 navel oranges
- 2 tangerines

How to Make

1. Combine sugar, ¼ cup tarragon, and ¼ cup water in a jar, cover, and shake until sugar is dissolved.

2. Strain tarragon syrup through a fine-mesh sieve into a clean jar or small bowl; discard tarragon.

3. Using a sharp knife, remove peel and white pith from blood oranges, clementines, navel oranges, and tangerines; discard. Slice citrus crosswise into ¼"-thick rounds.

4. Arrange citrus on a platter, drizzle with tarragon syrup (if your citrus is sweet, you may not want to use all of the syrup), and top with more tarragon leaves.▢

DINNER

Broiled Salmon with Spinach

Start to End: 15 minutes

Servings: 1

Ingredients

- 4 ounces fresh wild salmon
- 1 ½ tbsps Dijon mustard
- 2 tbsps low sodium soy sauce or Bragg Liquid Aminos
- 1 cup steamed spinach
- to taste salt
- to taste freshly ground black pepper

How to Make

1. Preheat broiler. Spread the top of the salmon with mustard and drizzle with soy sauce.
2. Place in a baking pan (sprayed liberally with cooking spray) and broil for 8-10 minutes, or until cooked through.
3. While the salmon is cooking, steam the spinach.
4. Top salmon with spinach and season with salt and pepper to taste. ⍰

DAY 7

BREAKFAST

Smoked Salmon, Avocado, and Poached Eggs on Toast

Start to End: 15 minutes

Servings: 2

Ingredients

- 2 slices of bread toasted
- 2 oz avocado smashed
- ¼ tsp freshly squeezed lemon juice
- Pinch of kosher salt and cracked black pepper
- oz smoked salmon
- 2 eggs, poached
- Splash of Kikkoman soy sauce optional
- 1 tbsp thinly sliced scallions

- Microgreens optional

How to Make

1. In a small bowl, smash the avocado. Add the lemon juice and a pinch of salt; mix well and set aside.
2. Poach your eggs and, when they are sitting in the ice bath, toast your bread.
3. Once your bread is toasted, spread the avocado on both slices and add the smoked salmon to each slice.
4. Carefully transfer the poached eggs to their respective toasts.
5. Hit with a splash of Kikkoman soy sauce and some cracked pepper; garnish with scallions and microgreens.

?

LUNCH

Rosemary Citrus One Pan Baked Salmon

Start to End: 20 minutes

Servings: 3

Ingredients

- 1/3 c olive oil
- Pinch of ground pepper
- 2 tbsp fresh orange juice
- 2 tbsp fresh rosemary, plus 1-2 extra sprigs to garnish
- 1 tbsp Lemon juice
- 1/2 tsp garlic minced
- 1/4 tsp of grated dried orange peel (divided)
- Kosher salt or fine sea salt to taste
- 1 bunch thin asparagus (trimmed)
- Olive oil or melted butter to drizzle

- 10–12 ounces sockeye salmon
- Thinly sliced Orange (5-6)
- Optional 1/4 tsp lemon pepper
- Additional Salt/pepper to taste – after baking

How to Make

1. Preheat oven to 400F.
2. Whisk together orange juice, lemon, 2 tbsp rosemary, 1/4 to 1/3 cup olive oil, pinch of salt, pepper, 1/4 tsp orange peel and garlic. Set aside.
3. Next Layer your dish.
4. First add your trimmed asparagus and drizzle with olive oil or butter. Add a pinch (1/4 tsp or so) of lemon pepper seasoning.
5. Place your salmon on between the asparagus spears.
6. Drizzle the orange rosemary marinade on top of the salmon.
7. Add thin orange slices on top of the salmon and on top of the asparagus.
8. Place 2 to 2 fresh sprigs of rosemary evenly on top of the salmon and around the pan.
9. Sprinkle a bit more orange peel, pepper, and kosher salt on top of the salmon veggie bake.
10. Bake at 400F for 12-15 minutes or until salmon is not longer opaque in the middle.

⁇

SNACK

Maple Sesame Quinoa Bars (Nut Free)

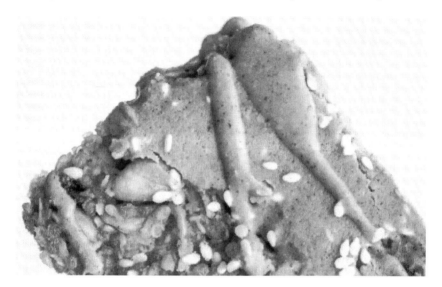

Start to End: 15 minutes

Servings: 14

Ingredients

- ¼ cup sesame seeds (toasted)
- 1/3 cup pumpkin seeds
- 1 cup gluten free rolled oats
- 3 cups cooked quinoa
- 1 tsp cinnamon
- 1/3 cup unsweetened shredded coconut
- 7 tbsp coconut oil, butter, or vegan butter (chopped)
- 1/3 cup maple syrup

- 1/3 to 1/2 cup sunflower seed butter for nut free option (or creamy peanut butter or almond butter)
- 1/3 cup coconut sugar
- 1 tsp vanilla

Shell Topping:

- 1/2 c sunflower seed butter or nut butter of choice.
- 1/4 c coconut oil
- pinch of cinnamon

How to Make

1. Preheat oven to 350°F. Line an 8×11 pan with parchment paper. (see notes for pan size options)
2. Place sesame seeds on baking sheet and toast in oven for about 5 minutes or until toasted lightly.
3. Next combine your dry ingredients. Place cooked Quinoa, gluten free oats, sesame seeds, pumpkin seeds, cinnamon, coconut, cooked quinoa, and in a large bowl. Mix all together. Set aside.
4. Place butter (or coconut oil), maple syrup, sunflower seed butter or nut butter of choice, coconut sugar, and vanilla in a small saucepan and cook over medium heat until butter and nut butter are melted.
5. Then turn heat to a quick boil for 1 minute. Reduce and simmer for 5 minutes until mix is thickened, stirring often.
6. Pour nut/seed sugar mixture into dry ingredients. Mix all together and then press firmly into pan; Place in refrigerator to set, covered.
7. While bars are setting, make your sunflower seed butter (or almond butter) shell. You don't have to use all of the shell coating if you prefer to make these bars less dense.

8. In a small sauce pan, mix together the 1/2 c sunflower seed butter (or nut butter), coconut oil, and 1 tsp cinnamon on medium heat until melted.

9. Pour this mix over your pan of bars and place back in refrigerator or freezer until set. Once set, slice bars and wrap each one in foil or wax paper to hold.

10. Store in fridge or freezer.

?

DINNER

Lentil and Chicken Soup with Sweet Potato

Start to End: 35 minutes

Servings: 6

Ingredients

- 1 cooked chicken carcass
- 1 lb. sweet potatoes, peeled, cut into 1" pieces
- 3/4 cup French lentils, rinsed
- 1 tsp. kosher salt, plus more
- 2 Tbsp. extra-virgin olive oil
- 10 celery stalks, sliced on the bias into 1/4" slices
- 6 garlic cloves, thinly sliced

- 1 1/2 cups shredded cooked chicken
- 1/2 head escarole, cut into bite-size pieces
- 1/2 cup finely chopped dill
- 2 tbsps fresh lemon juice

How to Make

1. Place chicken carcass, potatoes, lentils, and 1 tsp. salt in a large pot. Cover with 8 cups water. Bring to a boil over high heat, skimming off any foam, then reduce heat to medium-low and simmer until potatoes are fork tender and lentils are cooked through, 10–12 minutes. Discard chicken carcass.
2. Meanwhile, heat oil in a large heavy skillet over medium-high. Add celery and garlic and cook, stirring often, until celery and garlic are lightly golden brown and tender, about 12 minutes.
3. Stir celery, garlic, shredded chicken, and escarole into soup and cook, stirring occasionally, until escarole is wilted, about 5 minutes. Remove from heat.
4. Stir in dill and lemon juice; season soup with salt. ▨

DAY 8

BREAKFAST

Buckwheat and Chia Seed Porridge

Start to End:

Servings: 6

Ingredients

- 1 cup buckwheat, rinsed
- ½ cup oats
- 2 tbsps chia seeds
- 2 cups milk (cow's, almond or soy)
- 2 cups water
- 1 each pear and apple, grated with skin on
- 1 tsp each ground ginger and cinnamon
- ½ tsp each ground nutmeg and cardamom
- 2 tbsps nut butter

- 1 tsp vanilla extract
- 2 tbsps honey

Mixed Berry Compote:

- 500 grams mixed frozen berries
- finely grated zest and juice 1 orange
- ⅓ cup caster sugar
- 2 tsps corn flour
- 1 tbsp water

How to Make

1. Put the buckwheat and oats in a bowl and cover well with cold water. Put the chia seeds in a separate bowl and add 1 cup of the milk. Leave both bowls on the bench to soak overnight.
2. Drain the buckwheat and oats in a fine sieve then rinse well under cold water.
3. Place the chia seeds with the milk in a medium saucepan along with the remaining 1 cup milk, the buckwheat and oats, water, grated pear and apple, all the spices, nut butter, vanilla and honey.
4. Cook over a low heat for about 30 minutes, stirring often until thick and creamy, adding more water or milk to keep it at a soft consistency. Serve in bowls topped with your choice of toppings.
5. The porridge keeps well in the fridge for 5 days. Just heat each serving when needed, adding a little extra liquid if needed.

Mixed Berry Compote:

1. Put the berries, orange zest and juice and the caster sugar in a saucepan and slowly bring to the boil.

2. Mix the cornflour and water together in a bowl until smooth then stir into the berries.

3. Simmer for a couple of minutes until the juices have thickened. Serve warm or at room temperature. Makes about 2 cups

Topping:

1. Milk or cream or a non-dairy milk such as almond or soy; coconut yoghurt or regular yoghurt – plain or fruit; roasted figs with honey; fresh berries when in season; cinnamon-roasted pears or apples; poached rhubarb with raspberries; sliced banana and maple syrup; toasted nuts and seeds – almonds, macadamias, pecans, walnuts, hazelnuts, pistachios, sesame, sunflower and pumpkin seeds. ⏁

LUNCH

Cauliflower Steak with Beans and Tomatoes

Start to End: 45 minutes

Servings: 2

Ingredients

- 1 large head of cauliflower (about 2 pounds)
- ½ cup olive oil, divided
- 2 tsps kosher salt, divided
- 1 tsp freshly ground black pepper, divided
- 8 ounces green beans, trimmed
- 3 garlic cloves, finely chopped
- ¾ teaspoon finely grated lemon zest
- 1/3 cup chopped parsley, plus more for serving
- 1/3 cup panko (Japanese breadcrumbs)

- ¼ cup freshly grated Parmesan
- 1 (15-ounce) can white beans, rinsed, drained
- 1 cup golden or red cherry tomatoes (about 6 ounces), halved
- 3 tbsps mayonnaise
- 1 tsp Dijon mustard

How to Make

2. Arrange racks in middle and upper third of oven; preheat to 425°F. Remove leaves and trim stem end of cauliflower, leaving core intact.
3. Place cauliflower core side down on a work surface. Using a large knife, slice in the center from top to bottom to yield 2 (1") "steaks"; reserve remaining cauliflower for another use.
4. Place cauliflower on a rimmed baking sheet. Brush both sides with 1 Tbsp. oil; season with 1/4 tsp. salt and 1/4 tsp. pepper.
5. Roast on middle rack, turning halfway through, until cauliflower is tender and browned, about 30 minutes.
6. Meanwhile, toss green beans with 1 Tbsp. oil, 1/2 tsp. salt, and 1/4 tsp. pepper on another rimmed baking sheet.
7. Arrange in a single layer, then roast in upper third of oven until green beans begin to blister, about 15 minutes.
8. Whisk garlic, lemon zest, 1/3 cup parsley, and remaining 6 Tbsp. oil, 1 1/4 tsp. salt, and 1/2 tsp. pepper in a medium bowl until smooth.
9. Transfer half of mixture to another medium bowl. Add panko and Parmesan to first bowl and mix with your hands.
10. Add white beans and tomatoes to second bowl and toss to coat. Whisk mayonnaise and mustard in a small bowl.
11. Remove sheets from oven. Spread mayonnaise mixture over cauliflower. Sprinkle 1/4 cup panko mixture evenly over cauliflower.

12. Add white bean mixture to sheet with green beans and toss to combine. Return sheets to oven and continue to roast until white beans begin to crisp and panko topping starts to brown, 5–7 minutes more.
13. Divide cauliflower, green beans, white beans, and tomatoes among plates. Top with parsley.

SNACK

Citrus Salad with Greek Yogurt

Start to End: 20 minutes

Servings: 6

Ingredients

- 1 pink grapefruit, peeled
- 2 large tangerines or Minneolas, peeled
- 3 navel oranges
- 1/2 cup dried cranberries
- 2 tbsps honey
- 1/4 teaspoon ground cinnamon
- 1 16- or 17.6-ounce container Greek yogurt
- 2/3 cup minced crystallized ginger

- 1/4 cup golden brown sugar
- Additional dried cranberries

How to Make

1. Break grapefruit and tangerines into sections. Cut grapefruit sections into thirds; cut tangerine sections in half.
2. Transfer grapefruit, tangerines, and all juices to deep serving bowl.
3. Using small sharp knife, cut all peel and white pith from oranges. Slice oranges into 1/4-inch-thick rounds, then cut slices into quarters.
4. Add oranges and all juices to same bowl. Mix in 1/2 cup dried cranberries, honey, and cinnamon.
5. Cover and refrigerate at least 1 hour. Mix yogurt and ginger in bowl.
6. Spoon yogurt atop fruit. Sprinkle with brown sugar and dried cranberries.

DINNER

Vegetarian Chili

Start to End: 1 hour

Servings: 6

Ingredients

- 2 tbsps extra-virgin olive oil
- 1 medium red onion, chopped
- 1 large red bell pepper, chopped
- 2 medium carrots, chopped
- 2 ribs celery, chopped
- ½ tsp salt, divided
- 4 cloves garlic, pressed or minced
- 2 tablespoons chili powder*

- 2 tsps ground cumin
- 1 ½ tsps smoked paprika*
- 1 tsp dried oregano
- 1 large can or 2 small cans diced tomatoes, with their juices
- 2 cans black beans, rinsed and drained
- 1 can pinto beans, rinsed and drained
- 2 cups vegetable broth or water
- 1 bay leaf
- 2 tablespoons chopped fresh cilantro, plus more for garnishing
- 1 to 2 teaspoons sherry vinegar or red wine vinegar or lime juice, to taste

Garnishes:

- chopped cilantro
- sliced avocado
- tortilla chips
- sour cream or crème fraiche
- grated cheddar cheese.

How to Make

1. In a large oven or heavy-bottomed pot over medium heat, warm the olive oil until shimmering. Add the chopped onion, bell pepper, carrot, celery and ¼ teaspoon of the salt.
2. Stir to combine and cook, stirring occasionally, until the vegetables are tender and the onion is translucent, about 7 to 10 minutes.
3. Add the garlic, chili powder, cumin, smoked paprika and oregano. Cook until fragrant while stirring constantly, about 1 minute.
4. Add the diced tomatoes and their juices, the drained black beans and pinto beans, vegetable broth and bay leaf. Stir to

combine and let the mixture come to a simmer. Continue cooking, stirring occasionally and reducing heat as necessary to maintain a gentle simmer, for 30 minutes. Remove the chili from the heat.

5.   For the best texture and flavor, transfer 1 ½ cups of the chili to a blender, making sure to get some of the liquid portion. Securely fasten the lid and blend until smooth, then pour the blended mixture back into the pot.

6.   Add the chopped cilantro, stir to blend, and then mix in the vinegar, to taste. Add salt to taste, too—I added ¼ teaspoon more at this point. Divide the mixture into individual bowls and serve with garnishes of your choice. This chili will keep well in the refrigerator for about 4 days or you can freeze it for longer-term storage. ⏹

DAY 9

?

BREAKFAST

Turmeric Oatmeal

Start to End: 20 minutes

Servings: 1

Ingredients

Oatmeal:

- ½ cup Whole Rolled Oats
- 1 cup Water
- 1 splash Oat Milk or any other plant milk you like
- ½ tsp Turmeric Powder

Toppings:

- Raspberries
- Blueberries

- Mixed Seeds
- Flaked Almonds
- Dried Cranberries
- Desiccated Coconut
- Mint Leaves
- Maple Syrup (optional)

How to Make

1. Measure the oats, hemp milk, water and spices into a saucepan.
2. Cook over a medium to high heat for about 5 minutes, until it reaches you desired consistency.
3. Top up with raspberries, blueberries, almonds, cranberries and whatever you fancy.

LUNCH

Pickled Pineapple Baja Fish Tacos

Start to End: 50 minutes

Servings: 4

Ingredients

For the Quick Pickled Pineapple Relish:

- 1 c chopped pineapple
- (or 1/2 c pineapple and 1/2 c other tropical fruit)
- 1/4 c Apple Cider Vinegar
- 1/4 c coconut sugar
- 1/3 c water
- Pinch of ground mustard and paprika each
- Pinch fennel seed
- 1/4 tsp sea salt
- Pinch of Black pepper

- Optional – 2-3 tbsp chopped shallot or red onion
- Green onion to garnish

For the Baja Fish Tacos:

- 8 ounces cod, tilapia, or haddock (we use sizzlefish cod)
- avocado oil or butter
- 2 tbsp arrowroot starch or gluten free flour of choice
- 1/2 tsp minced garlic
- 1 tbsp chili sauce or blackened seasoning mix to taste (1–2 tsp)
- salt/pepper to taste
- 2 1/2 cups chopped red cabbage
- Fresh chopped cilantro
- 1 lime – juice (divided)
- 3–4 tbsp paleo mayonnaise
- 1/2 avocado
- Pinch of pepper, sea salt, garlic powder
- 4 gluten free tortillas
- optional red pepper flakes or sliced spicy pepper of choice to top.

How to Make

1. Make Pickled Pineapple Relish
2. In a small sauce pan, bring your pickling ingredients; Apple cider vinegar, water, sugar, ground mustard, paprika, salt/pepper, and fennel seed) to a boil.
3. Add the pineapple chunks to the pot and toss, coating it evenly. If you are wanting to add optional red onion, do so here.
4. Remove from stove to cool. Once cooled, place in a bowl, cover, and let it marinate in the fridge for at least 30 minutes. I

like to add a 1 tbsp of chopped green onion on top before refrigerating, but that's not required.

5. Once it's marinated, drain part of the excess juice from bowl (keep a few tablespoons), then place in food processor and pulse a few times to create a relish texture. Set aside while you make your baja tacos.

For the Baja Fish Tacos:

1. Clean your fish fillets then dice into small pieces.
2. Dredge the fish pieces in 1 to 2 tbsp oil, chili sauce or blackening seasoning, then arrowroot starch or flour. You can add extra chipotle powder or blackening spices again before frying, if desired.
3. Fry fish in oiled pan on medium high, turning fish while cooking for 5-6 minutes or until fish is cooked through. Add a squeeze of fresh lime and sea salt/pepper to taste.
4. After you cook the fish, quickly make your slaw with Avocado Cream (Crema)

For Avocado Crema:

1. Blend together 1/2 avocado with mayo or yogurt. Add salt, pepper, onion powder, Splash of lime juice, and mix again. You can either toss your cabbage in the Avocado Crema sauce or add it on top of the tacos. Both ways are delish. If you are not adding the Avocado Crema Sauce to the cabbage, just salt and pepper the slaw to taste before filling tacos.
2. Now layer your tacos!
3. Warm tortilla, cabbage slaw, Baja fish, and pineapple relish on top! Extra cilantro and chopped green onion to garnish.
4. Salt/Pepper to taste. Optional red pepper flakes or spicy pepper of choice to top! ⏑

SNACK

Trail Mix

Start to End: 2 minutes

Servings: 3

Ingredients

- 1 cup almonds
- 1 cup brazil nuts
- ¼ cup pumpkin seeds
- Handful goji berries
- Small sprinkle of toasted coconut flakes
- 2 sun-dried organic pineapple slices

How to Make

1. Combine all the ingredients and store in an airtight container in the fridge.
2. Divide into handful size portions and enjoy as a quick meal or healthy snack.

DINNER

Asian Zoodle Flu Buster Soup

Start to End: 20 minutes

Servings: 3

Ingredients

- 2 zucchini spiralizer about 1 pound or 3/4 lb. pressed to remove water
- 1 tbsp of sesame oil
- 1 tbsp fresh grated ginger
- 1 tsp minced garlic
- 1 tsp cumin
- ½ tsp anise seed
- ½ tsp crushed fennel seed
- Pinch of five spice or cinnamon
- Pinch of kosher salt

- Pinch of black Pepper
- 24 ounces vegetable or chicken broth
- 1 tbsp fish sauce or Tamari sauce (gluten free soy sauce)
- Optional 0 1 tbsp asian chili sauce
- 2 – 2 1/2 cups shredded or chopped red or purple cabbage (extra for topping)
- 1 tsp lime juice

Toppings and Garnishes :

- 3 –4 Eggs fried or scrambled (for plating)
- Sliced jalapeno or Thai red Pepper (both work and are delicious)
- handful of chopped Cilantro or thai basil (to garnish)
- 1–2 green onion stalks. Diced green portion
- 1 Lime (cut into wedges)
- Sesame seeds to garnish.
- Crushed salted nuts (cashews, almonds, or peanuts work great).
- sea salt and Black pepper to taste

How to Make

1. First, clean your zucchini and either spiralize or julianne cut. Press the zucchini between 2 paper towels and remove excess water. Place in a bowl for later.
2. In a medium sauce pan, heat the sesame over medium heat, add in your shallots, garlic, ginger and stir fry until lightly browned. About 1- 2 minutes.
3. While that is browning, crush your fennel seeds. You can do this with back of a knife. You just want to crush the fennel seeds to extract more of the flavor.

4. Add in the crushed seeds, cumin, anise, 5 spice, salt , broth, pepper and salt. Bring to a boil, stirring occasionally.
5. Mix in your fish sauce and optional chili sauce.
6. Next, add in chopped cabbage and simmer until the softened, about 2 to 3 minutes.
7. Add the zoodles, and bring to a quick boil again. Then reduce to low and simmer for another 2 minutes or until everything is cooked though and the broth is to your liking.
8. If you are adding egg as topping, do so now. Quickly scramble an egg in a small skillet or fry in 2 tsp oil.
9. Spoon soup into soup bowls and top with extra crunchy raw cabbage and cooked egg.
10. Garnish with sliced jalapeño or Thai red peppers, chopped cilantro, diced green onion, lime wedge, sesame seeds, crushed nuts, sea salt and black pepper. 🢒

DAY 10

☐

BREAKFAST

Red Velvet Smoothie

Start to End: 7 minutes

Servings: 2

Ingredients

- ½ cup chopped roasted beet root (approximately 1 small beet root) chilled or at room temperature
- 1 cup frozen cherries
- ½ cup raw cacao powder
- ½ cup coconut "cream" (see notes below)
- 1 cup chilled filtered water
- 1 cup ice

- 8 medjool dates, pitted
- ½ tsp pure vanilla extract
- 1 tsp gelatinized maca (optional)
- 1 tbsp pure maple syrup (optional)
- Pinch of Himalayan salt
- Puffed whole grain cereal for topping, optional

How to Make

1. Put all of the ingredients, except for the cereal, in the order listed above in a blender.
2. Process on high until smooth and creamy.
3. Divide into 2 cups and sprinkle the whole grain cereal (if using) on top. Serve at once.

LUNCH

Apple Kimchi Salad with Beef

Start to End: 30 minutes

Servings: 2

Ingredients

For the Apple Kimchi Salad:

- 2 apples (green and/or red). One of each is best combo!
- 1 small seedless cucumber
- green onion diced.
- 1 tbsp hot mustard (asian) or a Dijion mustard
- 1 tbsp chili sauce (ex chili paste or Sriracha).
- ¼ tsp pinch of paprika
- ¼ tsp sea salt
- 1 tbsp rice vinegar (rice wine vinegar)

- 1–2 tsp fresh grated fresh ginger or 1/4 to 1/2 tsp ground ginger
- Crushed black pepper to taste
- For the Garlic Sesame Beef:
- tsp oil (avocado or sesame oil for frying)
- tsp minced garlic (2–3 cloves minced)
- 1 tsp tamari sauce (Gluten Free soy sauce. Whole 30 option see notes)
- 6 – 8 oz organic lean beef (top round, steak, separable lean only, 95 % lean ground)
- 1 to 2 tbsp sesame seeds for topping (extra for garnishing and plating)
- sea salt and pepper to taste

Garnishes for the Salad:

- leafy greens
- sliced radish (1/2 cup)
- optional; crushed red pepper flakes
- optional; fresh cilantro

How to Make

1. First prepare your ⊡uick Apple kimchi Salad. Spiralize (or julienne slice) your apples. It's best to use a green and red to even out tartness with taste. But any apple will do if you don't have one of each.

2. Spiralize or julienne slice your cucumber. Place in a large bowl and press out any excess water with a paper towel. Set aside.

3. Chop your onion and garlic (if using cloves) and place in a small mixing bowl

4   Then add in your mustard, spices, chili sauce, vinegar, and lastly the ginger. Fresh always taste better but ground works fine too.

5   Toss kimchi flavored apple cucumber salad all together.

6   Place in fridge to marinate while you cook beef.

For the Beef:

1   Mix 2 tsp sesame oil, 1 tsp minced garlic, 2 tsp sesame seed, and dash of tamari in a small bowl. Whisk together and pour over your meat. Marinate for 10-20 minutes. Or skip if in a hurry.

2   Heat skillet to medium high.

3   Place your marinated steak (with oil) in the pan and sear for ingredients in a medium high for 7-10 minutes, turning. Or until beef is cooked to 140F and browned.

4   Remove from heat, strain excess fat/grease if desired.

5   Sprinkle with extra sesame see

The Bowl:

1   Divide the apple kimchi salad into two bowls.

2   Place a radish, sprouts, or green leaf on one side of the bowl.

3   Divide the beef strips (or ground) into the two bowls or plates.

4   Top beef with extra red pepper flakes and sesame seed if desired.

5   Drizzle any extra sauce on top of salad.

6   Garnish with cilantro. ☐

SNACK

Power Balls

Start to End: 45 minutes

Servings: 25

Ingredients

- ½ Cup puffed millet
- 1 cup puffed kamut or puffed rice
- ½ cup diced dried plums
- 1/3 cup semisweet chocolate chips
- ¼ cup sesame seeds
- 1/3 cup sunflower butter, at room temperature
- ½ cup honey
- ¾ cup shredded unsweetened coconut

How to Make

1   In a large bowl, toss together the puffed millet and puffed kamut or rice.
2   Add the dried plums, chocolate chips, and sesame seeds.
3   Stir in the sunflower butter and the honey. You should have a nice sticky mess!
4   Cover the bowl with plastic wrap and refrigerate for 30 minutes.
5   Place the coconut in a small bowl. Using a tablespoon, scoop the mixture and form it into 1-inch (2.5cm) balls with your hands.
6   Roll the balls in the coconut and transfer to a container.
7   You can store the power balls in the refrigerator for up to 1 week, or in the freezer in a zip-top freezer bag for up to 1 month, but I bet they won't last that long!

DINNER

Roasted Cauliflower, Fennel, and Ginger Soup

Start to End: 45 minutes

Servings: 2

Ingredients

- 1 red onion quartered
- 4 garlic cloves
- ½ head large cauliflower (cut into florets)
- 2 fennel bulbs chopped and cored
- 500 gms stock of choice
- 3 tbs hummus

- 1 TBS Golden Gut Blend   (or use 1 tsp tumeric and pinch cinnamon and black pepper)
- 1 tsp sage leaves
- pinch fennel seeds
- 2 tbs wheat free tamari
- 2 tbs lemon
- 1 knob ginger (peeled)

How to Make

1   Preheat oven to 200 degrees Celsius
2   On a baking tray place red onion, garlic cloves, cauliflower and the fennel.
3   Bake for 30-35 minutes until crispy.
4   Remove from the oven and place in a blender with remaining ingredients.
5   Blend until creamy.
6   Pour into heavy bottomed saucepan and place on stovetop.
7   Heat through on low to allow flavours to meld. Add season to taste.
8   Let cool slightly and serve warm.
9   Decorate with fennel fronds.

DAY 11

[?]

BREAKFAST

Golden Milk

Start to End: 5 minutes

Servings: 5

Ingredients

- 1 ½ cups light coconut milk (canned is best, but carton works too)
- 1 ½ cups unsweetened plain almond milk (DIY or store-bought)
- 1 ½ tsp ground turmeric
- ¼ tsp ground ginger
- 1 whole cinnamon stick
- 1 tbsp coconut oil

- 1 pinch ground black pepper
- Sweetener of choice (i.e. maple syrup, coconut sugar, or stevia to taste)

How to Make

1 To a small saucepan, add coconut milk, almond milk, ground turmeric, ground ginger, cinnamon stick, coconut oil, black pepper, and sweetener of choice

2 Whisk to combine and warm over medium heat. Heat until hot to the touch but not boiling - about 4 minutes - whisking freⱭuently.

3 Turn off heat and taste to adjust flavor. Add more sweetener to taste or more turmeric or ginger for intense spice + flavor.

4 Serve immediately, dividing between two glasses and leaving the cinnamon stick behind. Best when fresh, though leftovers can be stored covered in the refrigerator for 2-3 days. Reheat on the stovetop or microwave until hot.Ɑ

LUNCH

Lentil, Beetroot, and Hazelnut Salad

Start to End: 10 minutes

Servings: 3

Ingredients

For the salad:

- 1 cup Puy lentils, rinsed
- 2 3/4 cup filtered water
- Sea salt
- 3 cooked beetroot, cut into small cubes
- 2 spring onions, finely sliced
- 2 tbsps hazelnuts, roughly chopped
- A handful of fresh mint, roughly chopped
- A handful of fresh parsley, roughly chopped

For the ginger dressing:

- 3/4-inch cube of fresh ginger, peeled and roughly chopped
- tablepoons olive oil
- 1 teaspoon Dijon mustard
- 1 tablespoon apple cider vinegar
- Pinch of sea salt and freshly ground black pepper

How to Make

1. For the lentils, put them in a saucepan, cover with water, bring to a boil the reduce the heat and simmer for about 15–20 minutes, or until all the liquid has evaporated and the lentils are not mushy and still with a bite.
2. As soon as the lentils are cooked transfer them to a large bowl and leave to cool.
3. Once the lentils are cool, add the beetroot, spring onions, hazelnuts and herbs and stir until everything is combined.
4. For the dressing, put the ginger, mustard, oil and vinegar in a bowl and, using a hand-held blender, blend until combined.
5. Drizzle the dressing over the salad and serve.

?

SNACK

Chia Seed Pudding

Start to End: 10 minutes

Servings: 1

Ingredients

- One 13.5-ounce can light coconut milk
- 3 tablespoons chia seeds
- 3 tablespoons pure maple syrup
- 1/2 cup fresh pineapple chunks
- 2 medium kiwis, peeled and sliced
- 1/4 cup raspberries
- 2 tablespoons roasted almonds, chopped

How to Make

1. Special equipment: four 8-ounce glass jars with lids.

2. Stir together the coconut milk, chia seeds and maple syrup in a medium bowl.
3. Divide the mixture evenly among four 8-ounce glass jars.
4. Screw on the lids, and refrigerate overnight, covered, to allow the seeds to plump and the mixture to thicken into a loose pudding.
5. Arrange the pineapples, kiwis, raspberries and almonds in separate layers on top of the pudding.
6. Cover with the lid, and keep refrigerated for up to 1 day.⏴

DINNER

Sesame Shrimp Stir Fry

Start to End: 55 minutess

Servings: 4

Ingredients

- 2 cups water
- 1 cup uncooked white rice
- 1 pound medium shrimp, peeled and deveined
- ¼ tsp ground ginger
- ¼ tsp cayenne pepper
- 1 clove garlic, minced
- 1 tbsp sesame seeds
- ¼ tsp ground black pepper

- 2 tbsps sesame oil
- 1 red bell pepper, sliced into thin strips
- 3 green onions, sliced
- 3 tbsps teriyaki sauce
- ½ pound sugar snap peas
- 1/8 cup cornstarch
- 3/4 cup chicken broth

How to Make

1. In a medium saucepan, bring salted water to a boil. Add rice, reduce heat, cover and simmer for 20 minutes.
2. While rice is simmering, combine shrimp, ginger, cayenne pepper, garlic, sesame seeds and black pepper in a large plastic food storage bag. Allow to marinate in the refrigerator.
3. Heat sesame oil in a large wok or skillet. Add red bell pepper and green onions; saute 3 to 4 minutes to soften slightly Add teriyaki sauce. Add peas and shrimp with seasoning; saute 4 minutes or until shrimp are opaue.
4. Stir cornstarch into chicken broth and add to wok; cook, stirring until mixture boils. Sprinkle with salt. Spoon shrimp mixture over rice.

DAY 12

BREAKFAST

Chai Spiced Chia Smoothie Bowls

Start to End: 1 hour 5 minutes

Servings: 2

Ingredients

- 16 oz coconut or almond drinking milk
- 2 chai tea bags (or see this bowl recipe for homemade chai spices)
- 1–2 tsp turmeric
- pinch of cinnamon
- 1 tbsp maple syrup or raw honey
- 2 + tbsp chia seed (divided)
- 1 tbsp almond butter

Optional thickeners:

- 1/4 cup gluten free oats
- 1 large frozen bananas (optional)
- 2–3 Frozen coconut milk cubes or ice cubs (optional, for thickness)
- Optional protein – 1 scoops plant protein powder or collagen.

How to Make

1. First heat your milk on stove top or in microwave. Place chai tea, turmeric, and cinnamon in pot or heat resistant jar and steep for 3-4 minutes. If using stove top, let the milk come to a quick boil then reduce and simmer for 2-3 minutes, 4 minutes all together.
2. Remove tea bags and whisk together.
3. Pour chai turmeric latte li?uid mixture into a blender along with 1 tbsp chia, honey or maple syrup, almond butter, optional oats (omit for paleo option), banana, and protein.
4. Blend together and pour into large jar.
5. Mix in the extra 1 tbsp chia seed (add an extra 1 tbsp if you want a chia pudding like texture). *See notes
6. Place jar in fridge to cool and thicken; 1 hour up to overnight.
7. Pour smoothie into 2 bowls and top with more cinnamon, and chia or oats (if desired). ?

LUNCH

Cooked Spinach and Pine Nuts

Start to End: 10 minutes

Servings: 1

Ingredients

- 3 pounds spinach
- 2 tsps olive oil
- 2 tbsps pine nuts, toasted
- 1 tsp garlic, minced
- to taste freshly ground black pepper

How to Make

1. Wash spinach allowing water to cling to leaves.
2. Heat oil in skillet over medium-high heat.

---

3. Cook spinach until it wilts in skillet over medium-high heat, about 3 minutes.
4. Add pine nuts, and garlic and cook for 2 minutes.
5. Season with pepper and serve. ▢

SNACK

No Bake Lemon Coconut Paleo Energy Bars

Start to End: 10 minutes

Servings: 12

Ingredients

For the Bar Base:

- Parchment paper or wax paper to line pan
- 1 2/3 cup slivered almonds (blanched) or 1 3/4 cups raw almonds (whole).
- 1 cup raw cashews
- 1 cup unsweetened coconut flakes (to grind)
- 1 tbsp starch (arrowroot or tapioca work best)
- 1/4 cup hot water

- 1/4 cup honey or maple syrup
- Lemon zest
- Optional Lemon juice (1 tbsp)
- 1 tsp vanilla
- Optional lemon extract 1/2 tsp
- tbsp ground flaxseeds
- All ground then mixed with water/honey and pressed into lined 8×8 pan.

Topping:

- 1/3 cup unsweetened coconut flakes
- Lemon zest/peel
- 1/2 to 1 tsp coconut oil

How to Make

1. First line an 8×8 pan with parchment paper or wax paper. Set aside.
2. In a food processor or blender, grind your almonds and cashews into a finer mealy texture.
3. Next add in your coconut and blend again until batter is once again, mealy in texture. Pour batter in a large bowl and mix in your starch and 1 tbsp lemon zest.
4. Heat 1/4 cup of water in a heat safe container. Mix your honey, vanilla, and lemon extract or juice into the hot water.
5. Pour the hot water/lemon mixture into the coconut/lemon nut mixture.
6. Mix all together with spoon or hands. Add your ground flaxseed (or protein of choice) last.
7. Press batter into pan, evenly.
8. Finally, make your topping.

Topping and Storage tips:

1 Grind 1/3 cup unsweetened coconut flakes into a finer
   mixture. You can also just use shredded unsweetened
   coconut.
2 Mix this with a 3 thinly cut and chopped lemon slices or 1 tbsp
   lemon zest. and 1/2 to 1 tsp coconut oil. Mix or grind together
   again. Spread this mixture of the bars. If you are not looking
   for lower sugar option, feel free to drizzle Optional honey on
   top.
3 Place pan in fridge for 30 minutes or longer. Once set, remove
   from fridge and cut into 9-12 squares. Wrap individually and
   keep in fridge for up to 2 weeks or freezer for up to 6 weeks. ▨

DINNER

Black "Fried" Rice with Snap Peas and Scallions

Start to End: 20 minutes

Servings: 4

Ingredients

- 2 tbsps Organic Extra Virgin Coconut Oil
- 2 medium carrots diced
- 1 bunch scallions white and green parts separated, thinly sliced
- 1 cup thinly sliced snap peas
- 2 garlic cloves minced
- 1 tbsp minced fresh ginger

- cups cooked U.S.-grown black japonica rice from 1 cup uncooked
- 3 tbsps gluten-free tamari
- 2 tsps toasted sesame oil
- 1 teaspoon sriracha
- 2 eggs beaten
- 1 tbsp Organic Shelled Hemp Seed

How to Make

1 In a large wok or nonstick skillet heat the coconut oil. Sauté the carrot and white scallion over high heat until soft and beginning to brown, about 5 minutes.
2 Add the snap peas, garlic, ginger, and green scallions and stir-fry until fragrant, another 2 minutes.
3 Fold in the black japonica rice and stir-fry until well-coated in the vegetable mixture and beginning to toast, 2 minutes.
4 Add the gluten-free tamari, sesame oil, and sriracha and stir to combine.
5 Push the rice to the side of the pan to create a well. Pour the eggs into the center and cook, stirring gently, until nearly set.
6 Toss the fried rice with the eggs and hemp seeds. Transfer the fried rice to bowls and serve right away. ▧

DAY 13

?

BREAKFAST

Cherry Coconut Porridge

Start to End: 10 minutes

Servings: 1

Ingredients

- 1.5cups oats
- 4 tbsps chia seed
- 3-4 cups of coconut drinking milk
- 3 tbsps raw cacao
- pinch of stevia
- coconut shavings
- cherries (fresh or frozen)
- dark chocolate shavings
- maple syrup

How to Make

1   Combine oats, chia, coconut milk, cacao and stevia in a saucepan.
2   Bring to a boil over medium heat and then simmer over lower heat until oats are cooked.
3   Pour into a bowl and top with coconut shavings, cherries, dark chocolate shavings and maple syrup to taste. ⬚

LUNCH

Cranberry Walnut Salad

Start to End: 8 minutes

Servings: 6

Ingredients

- 2 tbsps olive oil
- 1 tbsp cider vinegar
- ½ tsp agave or honey
- 1 package mesclun greens
- 1 large head frisee, trimmed and torn into bite-size pieces
- 2 tbsps unsweetened, dried cranberries
- 2 tbsps raw walnut pieces
- 1 apple, sliced

How to Make

1   In a medium bowl, whisk together oil, vinegar, and agave or honey. Add mesclun greens and frisee. Toss to coat.
2   Top with cranberries and walnuts. Season with salt and pepper, if desired. ⊡

SNACK

Chia Seed Pudding

Start to End: 10 minutes

Servings: 1

Ingredients

- One 13.5-ounce can light coconut milk
- 3 tablespoons chia seeds
- 3 tablespoons pure maple syrup
- 1/2 cup fresh pineapple chunks
- 2 medium kiwis, peeled and sliced
- 1/4 cup raspberries
- 2 tablespoons roasted almonds, chopped

How to Make

1   Special equipment: four 8-ounce glass jars with lids.

2   Stir together the coconut milk, chia seeds and maple syrup in a medium bowl.

3   Divide the mixture evenly among four 8-ounce glass jars.

4   Screw on the lids, and refrigerate overnight, covered, to allow the seeds to plump and the mixture to thicken into a loose pudding.

5   Arrange the pineapples, kiwis, raspberries and almonds in separate layers on top of the pudding.

6   Cover with the lid, and keep refrigerated for up to 1 day.

DINNER

Curried Potatoes with Poached Eggs

Start to End: 40 minutes

Servings: 4

Ingredients

- russet potatoes
- 1 inch fresh ginger
- 2 cloves garlic
- 1 tbsp olive oil
- 2 tbsp curry powder (hot or mild)
- 15 oz can tomato sauce
- large eggs
- 1/2 bunch fresh cilantro (optional)

How to Make

1   Wash the potatoes well, then cut into 3/4-inch cubes. Place the cubed potatoes in a large pot and cover with water. Cover the pot with a lid and bring it up to a boil over high heat.

2   Boil the potatoes for 5-6 minutes, or until they're tender when pierced with a fork. Drain the cooked potatoes in a colander.

3   While the potatoes are boiling, begin the sauce. Peel the ginger with a vegetable peeler or scrape the skin off with the side of a spoon.

4   Use a small holed cheese grater to grate about one inch of ginger (less if you prefer a more subtle ginger flavor). Mince the garlic.

5   Add the ginger, garlic, and olive oil to a large, deep skillet (or a wide based pot). Sauté the ginger and garlic over medium low heat for 1-2 minutes, or just until soft and fragrant.

6   Add the curry powder to the skillet and sauté for about a minute more to toast the spices.

7   Add the tomato sauce to the skillet and stir to combine. Turn the heat up to medium and heat the sauce through. Taste the sauce and add salt, if needed.

8   Add the cooked and drained potatoes to the skillet and stir to coat in the sauce. Add a couple tablespoons of water if the mixture seems dry or pasty.

9   Create four small wells or dips in the potato mixture and crack an egg into each. Place a lid on the skillet and let it come up to a simmer. Simmer the eggs in the sauce for 6-10 minutes, or until cooked through. Top with chopped fresh cilantro. ☑

DAY 14

BREAKFAST

Yogurt Parfaits with Raspberries and Chia Seeds

Start to End: 10 minutes

Servings: 2

Ingredients

- ½ cup fresh raspberries
- tbsps chia seeds
- 1 tsp maple syrup
- Pinch of cinnamon
- 16-ounces plain yogurt
- Fresh fruit, such as sliced blackberries, nectarines, strawberries

How to Make

1. Place the raspberries in a small mixing bowl. Using the back of a fork, mash the berries until they reach a jam-like consistency.
2. Add the chia seeds, honey, and cinnamon to the bowl.
3. Continue to mash until all of the ingredients are fully incorporated. Set aside.
4. Place a layer of yogurt in the bottom of a medium-size glass or jar. Top with a layer of the raspberry chia mixture.
5. Finish with an additional layer of yogurt. Garnish with fresh sliced fruit and an extra drizzle of maple syrup, if desired. Repeat with the second glass/jar. ⏎

LUNCH

Detox Broccoli Salad without Mayo

Start to End: 30 minutes

Servings: 4

Ingredients

- 1 lb broccoli florets
- tsp to 3 tsp coconut oil or avocado oil
- Optional 1/2 tsp everything seasoning of choice (dried herbs, red pepper, etc.)
- 1/3 c to 1/2 c cultured plain yogurt or kefir yogurt (see notes for doubling sauce)
- 2 tsp red wine vinegar
- 1 garlic clove or 1/2 tsp minced
- Kosher Salt and Black pepper to taste

- 1/2 to 1 tbsp tbsp olive oil
- 1 tsp Lemon juice
- 1/2 c diced red onion or shallot
- 1 cup blueberries
- 1/4 cup roasted sunflower seeds
- 2 cups spinach leaves
- Fresh Cilantro or Parsley to garnish
- Peppercorns or fresh pepper and optional red pepper flakes.

How to Make

1. Preheat oven to 425F.
2. Toss half the broccoli florets (around 2 cups) in 2-3 tsp oil and seasoning of choice. Place on baking sheet and place in oven to roast for 20-25 minutes.
3. Place the other 1/2 lbs broccoli florets in a large mixing bowl. If you don't want to roast half, just toss all raw broccoli florets in a large bowl.
4. While broccoli is cooking, make your yogurt sauce.

For Yogurt Sauce:

1. Mix the yogurt, vinegar, garlic, salt/pepper, olive oil, lemon juice, and onion in a small bowl. Set aside.
2. Broccoli Salad
3. Place roasted broccoli and raw broccoli in one bowl. Mix in your blueberries, sunflower seeds, and spinach. Toss all together.
4. Next spoon your yogurt sauce over the broccoli and blueberry spinach salad. Toss all together.
5. Garnish with extra herbs (Cilantro or Parsley), peppercorn or pepper, and a pinch of red pepper if desired. ⯑

SNACK

Rosemary-Tangerine Cooler

Start to End: 10 minutes

Servings: 2

Ingredients

- 2 tbsps raw sugar plus more
- 2 tangerines, halved crosswise
- 16 rosemary sprigs, divided
- 2 cups white rum

How to Make

1   Heat a cast-iron skillet or griddle over high heat, or on a grill grate. Pour some raw sugar into a small plate. Dip cut sides of tangerines into sugar.

2   Scatter 8 rosemary sprigs in skillet; add tangerines, cut side down.

3   Cook until sugar caramelizes, about 2 minutes. Let cool.

4   Quarter tangerines; discard rosemary. Place tangerines in a pitcher, add 2 tbsp. raw sugar, and muddle to release juices. Add rum and 6 cups ice; stir until pitcher is frosty.

5   Divide among glasses; garnish with remaining 8 rosemary sprigs. ⬜

DINNER

Moroccan Red Lentil Soup with Chard

Start to End: 35 minutes

Servings: 4

Ingredients

- tbsps olive oil
- 1 medium yellow onion diced
- 2 medium carrots diced
- 2 large cloves garlic minced
- 1 tsp ground cumin
- ½ tsp ground ginger
- ½ tsp ground turmeric
- ½ tsp red chili flakes
- 1 tsp sea salt

- One 15-ounce can diced tomatoes
- 1 cup dried split red lentils
- 2 quarts vegetable stock
- 1 bunch chard stems removed, roughly chopped

How to Make

1   In a large stockpot or Dutch oven, heat the oil. Saute the onion and carrot over medium-high heat until soft and beginning to brown, 7 minutes.
2   Add the garlic, cumin, ginger, turmeric, chili flakes, and salt.
3   Cook one minute more.
4   Stir in the tomatoes, scraping up any brown bits from the bottom of the pan, and cook until the liquid has reduced and the tomatoes are soft, 5 minutes.
5   Add the lentils and stock. Bring to a boil, then reduce the heat and simmer uncovered until the lentils are soft, 10 minutes.
6   Fold in the chard and cook until wilted, but still vibrant, 5 more minutes. Taste for seasoning.
7   Serve the soup in bowls with a wedge of lemon on the side or a dollop of Greek yogurt. ⏷

DAY 15

?

BREAKFAST

Raspberry Smoothie

Start to End: 6 minutes

Servings: 2

Ingredients

- 1 ½ cups apple juice
- 1 banana
- 1 ½ cups frozen raspberries
- ¾ cup vanilla Greek yogurt
- 1 tbsp honey
- fresh raspberries and mint sprigs for garnish optional

How to Make

1   Place the apple juice, banana, raspberries, yogurt and honey into a blender.

2   Blend until smooth.

3   Pour into 2 glasses and serve, topped with raspberries and mint sprigs if desired. ⏹

LUNCH

Quinoa and Citrus Salad

Start to End: 10 minutes

Servings: 1

Ingredients

- 1 cup cooked ?uinoa, cooled
- 2 small oranges, supremed
- 1 celery rib, finely chopped
- 20g Brazil nuts, chopped
- 1 green onion, sliced
- ¼ cup fresh parsley, finely chopped

For the Dressing:

- juice from above oranges

- ½ tsp lemon juice
- ½ tsp fresh ginger, grated
- 1 tsp white wine vinegar
- 1 small clove garlic, minced
- ½ tsp salt
- ¼ tsp black pepper
- pinch cinnamon

How to Make

1. Cut the oranges into supremes, working over a bowl, in order not lose any of the juice.
2. When you've got all your supremes done, make sure to squeeze all the juice out of the "membranes" that are left behind.
3. Transfer that juice to your mini blender or food processor.
4. Add the rest of the ingredients for the dressing and blend until smooth.
5. Cut your orange supremes into bite size pieces and add them to a medium size mixing bowl. Add the rest of the ingredients, including the dressing, and stir until well combined.
6. Serve immediately, or keep in the refrigerator until ready to serve.

SNACK

Apple Chips

Start to End: 1 hour 30 minutes

Servings: 6

Ingredients

3   Golden Delicious apples, cored and thinly sliced
1   1 ½ tsps white sugar
2   ½ tsp ground cinnamon

How to Make

1   Preheat oven to 225 degrees F (110 degrees C).
2   Arrange apples slices on a metal baking sheet.
3   Mix sugar and cinnamon together in a bowl; sprinkle over apple slices.

4   Bake in the preheated until apples are dried and edges curl up, 45 minutes to 1 hour.

5   Transfer apple chips, using a metal spatula, to a wire rack until cooled and crispy. ⬚

DINNER

Slow Cooker Turkey Chili

Start to End: 4 hours 20 minutes

Servings: 8

Ingredients

- 1 tbsp olive oil
- 1 lb 99% lean ground turkey
- 1 medium onion diced
- 1 red pepper chopped
- 1 yellow pepper chopped
- (15 oz) cans tomato sauce
- 2 (15 oz) cans petite diced tomatoes
- 2 (15 oz) cans black beans, rinsed and drained
- 2 (15 oz) cans red kidney beans, rinsed and drained

- 1 (16 oz) jar deli-sliced tamed jalapeno peppers, drained
- 1 cup frozen corn
- 2 tbsps chili powder
- 1 tbsp cumin
- Salt and black pepper to taste

Optional Toppings:

- green onions shredded cheese
- avocado
- sour cream/Greek yogurt

How to Make

1. Heat the oil in a skillet over medium heat. Place turkey in the skillet, and cook until brown. Pour turkey into slow cooker.
2. Add the onion, peppers, tomato sauce, diced tomatoes, beans, jalapeños, corn, chili powder, and cumin. Stir and season with salt and pepper.
3. Cover and cook on High for 4 hours or low for 6 hours. Serve with toppings, if desired.
4. Make use of a 6 quart slow cooker.

DAY 16

☐

BREAKFAST

Rhubarb, Apple, and Ginger Muffins

Start to End: 30 minutes

Servings: 8

Ingredients

- ½ cup almond meal (ground almonds)
- ¼ cup unrefined raw sugar
- tbsps finely chopped crystallised ginger
- 1 tbsp ground linseed meal
- 1/2 cup buckwheat flour
- 1/4 cup fine brown rice flour
- 2 tbsps organic cornflour or true arrowroot
- 2 tsps gluten-free baking powder

- 1/2 tsp ground cinnamon
- 1/2 tsp ground ginger
- a good pinch fine sea salt
- 1 cup finely sliced rhubarb
- 1 small apple, peeled, cored and finely diced
- 95ml (1/3 cup + 1 tablespoon) rice or almond milk
- 1/4 cup (60ml) olive oil
- 1 large free-range egg
- 1 teaspoon vanilla extract

How to Make

1. Preheat oven to 180C/350C. Grease or line eight 1/3 cup (80ml) cup capacity muffin tins with paper cases.
2. Place almond meal, sugar, ginger and linseed meal into a medium bowl.
3. Sieve over flours, baking powder and spices, then whisk to combine evenly.
4. Stir in rhubarb and apple to coat in the flour mixture. In another smaller bowl whisk milk, oil, egg and vanilla before pouring into the dry mixture and stirring until just combined.
5. Evenly divide batter between tins/paper cases (scatter with a few slices of rhubarb if desired) and bake for 20-25 minutes or until risen, golden around the edges and when a skewer is inserted into the centre it comes out clean.
6. Remove from the oven and set aside for 5 minutes before transferring to a wire rack to cool further.
7. Eat warm or at room temperature Best eaten on the day of baking, however they will store in an airtight container for 2-3 days or frozen in zip-lock bags for longer. ☐

LUNCH

Rosemary Citrus One Pan Baked Salmon

Start to End: 20 minutes

Servings: 3

Ingredients

- 1/3 c olive oil
- Pinch of ground pepper
- tbsp fresh orange juice
- tbsp fresh rosemary, plus 1-2 extra sprigs to garnish
- 1 tbsp Lemon juice
- 1/2 tsp garlic minced
- 1/4 tsp of grated dried orange peel (divided)
- Kosher salt or fine sea salt to taste

- 1 bunch thin asparagus (trimmed) (Or other vegetable of choice)
- Olive oil or melted butter to drizzle
- 10–12 ounces sockeye salmon (whole fillet or around 3 fillets)
- Thinly sliced Orange (5-6)
- Optional 1/4 tsp lemon pepper
- Additional Salt/pepper to taste – after baking

How to Make

1. Preheat oven to 400F.
2. Whisk together orange juice, lemon, 2 tbsp rosemary, 1/4 to 1/3 cup olive oil, pinch of salt, pepper, 1/4 tsp orange peel and garlic. Set aside.
3. Next Layer your dish.
4. First add your trimmed asparagus (or other vegetable of choice) and drizzle with olive oil or butter. Add a pinch (1/4 tsp or so) of lemon pepper seasoning.
5. Place your salmon (skin side down) on between the asparagus spears.
6. Drizzle the orange rosemary marinade on top of the salmon.
7. Add thin orange slices on top of the salmon and on top of the asparagus.
8. Place 2 to 2 fresh sprigs of rosemary evenly on top of the salmon and around the pan.▢

SNACK

Raw Veggies with Homemade Vegan Ranch Dressing

Start to End: 10 minutes

Servings: 11

Ingredients

- 1/3 cup cashews (raw or dry roasted)
- ¾ cup unsweetened plain dairy-free milk beverage, plus additional as needed
- ½ cup olive oil, avocado oil, or grapeseed oil
- tsps lemon juice
- tsps apple cider vinegar

- Optional 1 tsp maple syrup or honey if not vegan (can substitute agave nectar) – Omit for Whole 30 option
- 1 tsp sea salt
- ½ tsp ground mustard
- ½ tsp onion powder
- ¼ to ½ tsp garlic powder
- ¼ tsp black pepper
- 2 tsps dried parsley or 1/4 cup chopped fresh parsley

For the platter:

- Vegetables of choice, sliced. E.g Carrots, celery, broccoli, grape tomatoes, etc.
- Herbs and lemon slices to garnish
- Optional gluten free or paleo friendly crackers

How to Make

1. Put the cashews in your spice grinder or small food processor and whiz until powdered, about 30 to 60 seconds.
2. Put the cashew powder, milk beverage, oil, lemon juice, vinegar, honey or maple syrup, salt, mustard, onion powder, garlic powder, and pepper in your blender and blend for 2 minutes.
3. It should emulsify and thicken slightly. Stir in the parsley.
3. Pour the dressing into an airtight bottle or container, cover, and refrigerator for at least 30 minutes to thicken and let the flavors develop.
4. Store in the refrigerator for up to 1 week.
5. Shake or whisk the dressing before each use. Makes 1 1/2 cups.

Arrange your snack platter:

1. Place 1/2 cup to 2/3 cup of vegan ranch in a small bowl. Place on large serving plate and then add fresh vegetables and/or crackers around it.
2. Garnish with lemon slices and herbs. Cracked pepper on top of ranch if desired. ⏸

DINNER

Italian-Style Stuffed Red Peppers

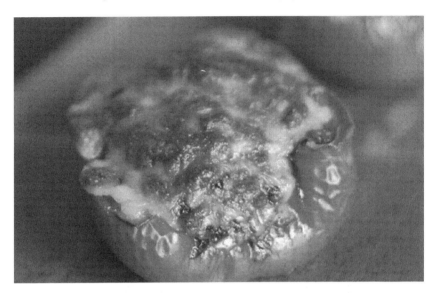

Start to End: 40 minutes

Servings: 3

Ingredients

- 1lb Lean ground turkey (Or lean ground beef)
- Red bell peppers
- cups Spaghetti sauce
- 1 tsp Basil/oregano seasoning (or any blend of italian herbs)
- 1tsp Garlic powder (or 1 garlic clove, pressed)
- 1/2 tsp Salt and pepper
- 1/2 cup Frozen chopped spinach (or veggie of choice)

- tbs Grated parmesan cheese + 6 tbs to garnish over the top of each pepper
- Optional 1 tsp (or 1 packet) low calorie sweetener of choice to put in the sauce

How to Make

1 Pre-heat oven to 450 degrees.
2 Line baking sheet with foil, (for easy clean up), coat with non-stick cooking spray.
3 Wash red peppers, and cut around the stem to remove.
4 Remove the stems. ⬚

DAY 17

?

BREAKFAST

Strawberry Veggie Smoothie

Start to End: 5 minutes

Servings: 5

Ingredients

- cups strawberries (fresh of frozen)
- 1 cup frozen cauliflower
- 1 large zucchini
- 1 tablespoon nut butter
- cups unsweetened vanilla almond milk
- 1 scoop vanilla protein powder
- 1 large handful ice

How to Make

1. Blend all ingredients in a high-speed blender until smooth. ⏱

LUNCH

Kale Caesar Salad with Grilled Chicken Wrap

Start to End: 10 minutes

Servings: 2

- Ingredients
- 8 ounces grilled chicken, thinly sliced
- 6 cups curly kale, cut into bite sized pieces
- 1 cup cherry tomatoes, quartered
- 3/4 cup finely shredded Parmesan cheese
- ½ coddled egg (cooked about 1 minute)
- 1 clove garlic, minced
- 1/2 tsp Dijon mustard
- 1 teaspoon honey or agave

- 1/8 cup fresh lemon juice
- 1/8 cup olive oil
- Kosher salt and freshly ground black pepper
- 2 Lavash flat breads or two large tortillas

How to Make

1. In a bowl, mix together the half of a coddled egg, minced garlic, mustard, honey, lemon juice and olive oil. Whisk until you have formed a dressing. Season to taste with salt and pepper.
2. Add the kale, chicken and cherry tomatoes and toss to coat with the dressing and ¼ cup of the shredded parmesan.
3. Spread out the two lavash flatbreads. Evenly distribute the salad over the two wraps and sprinkle each with ¼ cup of parmesan.
4. Roll up the wraps and slice in half. Eat immediately

SNACK

Lemon Turmeric Energy Balls

Start to End: 10 minutes

Servings: 24

Ingredients

- 12 Medjool dates
- 1 cup rolled oats gluten free
- ½ cup almonds
- 1 tbsp chia seeds
- tbsps lemon juice
- 1 tsp lemon zest
- 1 tsp vanilla extract
- 1 tsp turmeric powder
- Pinch of black pepper
- ½ cup shredded coconut for dusting

How to Make

1 Remove the pits from dates and soak them in hot water for several minutes.
2 When the dates are softened, drain them and place in food processor. Save the water.
3 Add the other ingredients to a food processor and blend until mixture turns into a dough-like consistency.
4 Add 1 tablespoon of water in which you have soaked the dates if the mixture is too dry.
5 With the small spoon scoop the mixture and roll into balls. Roll the balls in shredded coconut and place on the baking sheet.
6 Store energy balls in an airtight container in the refrigerator until serving. ⏹

DINNER

Cooked Spinach and Pine Nuts

Start to End: 10 minutes

Servings: 1

Ingredients

- pounds spinach
- teaspoons olive oil
- tablespoons pine nuts, toasted
- 1 teaspoon garlic, minced
- to taste freshly ground black pepper

How to Make

1 Wash spinach allowing water to cling to leaves.
2 Heat oil in skillet over medium-high heat.

3   Cook spinach until it wilts in skillet over medium-high heat, about 3 minutes.

4   Add pine nuts, and garlic and cook for 2 minutes.

5   Season with pepper and serve. ⏷

DAY 18

[?]

BREAKFAST

Green Tea Latte Overnight Oats

Start to End: 7 minutes

Servings: 2

Ingredients

- 1 cup old-fashioned rolled oats (gluten-free if desired)
- 1 tbsp chia seeds
- 1 tbsp hemp seeds
- 1 cup packed baby spinach
- 1 cup strong green tea, cooled to room temperature
- ½ cup unsweetened almond milk
- tbsps cashews, soaked in water overnight or for at least 1 hour*
- ¼ tsp cinnamon
- ½ tsp vanilla

- medjool dates, pits removed

Optional Toppings

- fresh berries
- sliced bananas
- cashews
- additional hemp seeds

How to Make

1 Add the oats, chia, and hemp seeds to a medium-large bowl and mix.
2 Drain the cashews and add them and all remaining ingredients (besides toppings) to a blender and blend until smooth.
3 Pour the blender mix into the bowl with the oats, chia, and hemp and mix. Cover and let sit in the refrigerator overnight.
4 In the morning, divide the oats between two bowls, top with seeds, bananas, berries, or additional nuts and enjoy! ▯

LUNCH

Red Quinoa Salad

Start to End: 1 hour 20 minutes

Servings: 4

Ingredients

- 1 cup uncooked red quinoa
- 1/3 cup olive oil
- tbsps red wine vinegar
- 1 ½ tsps finely minced shallots
- ¼ tsp kosher salt
- ¼ tsp freshly ground black pepper
- cups diced seeded tomato
- 1/2 cup diced seeded cucumber

- tbsps chopped fresh mint 1 tablespoon chopped fresh oregano
- 1 can chickpeas (garbanzo beans), rinsed and drained
- 2 ounces crumbled feta cheese (about 1/2 cup)
- lemon wedges

How to Make

1 Cook ⬚uinoa according to package directions, omitting salt and fat. Drain and place in a large bowl. Let cool 1 hour.
2 While ⬚uinoa cools, combine oil and next 4 ingredients (through pepper) in a small bowl, stirring with a whisk. Let stand 20 minutes.
3 Add dressing, tomato, and next 4 ingredients (through chickpeas) to ⬚uinoa; toss well. Add cheese, and toss gently. Serve with lemon wedges.
4 You can chop the tomatoes and cucumber, and then crumble the feta. ⬚

SNACK

Chia Seed Pudding

Start to End: 10 minutes

Servings: 1

Ingredients

- One 13.5-ounce can light coconut milk
- 3 tablespoons chia seeds
- 3 tablespoons pure maple syrup
- 1/2 cup fresh pineapple chunks
- 2 medium kiwis, peeled and sliced
- 1/4 cup raspberries
- 2 tablespoons roasted almonds, chopped

How to Make

1 Special equipment: four 8-ounce glass jars with lids.

2   Stir together the coconut milk, chia seeds and maple syrup in a medium bowl.
3   Divide the mixture evenly among four 8-ounce glass jars.
4   Screw on the lids, and refrigerate overnight, covered, to allow the seeds to plump and the mixture to thicken into a loose pudding.
5   Arrange the pineapples, kiwis, raspberries and almonds in separate layers on top of the pudding.
6   Cover with the lid, and keep refrigerated for up to 1 day.▢

DINNER

Baked Tilapia with Pecan Rosemary Topping

Start to End: 35 minutes

Servings: 4

Ingredients

- 1/3 cup chopped raw pecans
- 1/3 cup whole wheat panko breadcrumbs
- 2 tsps chopped fresh rosemary
- ½ tsp coconut palm sugar or brown sugar
- 1/8 tsp salt
- 1 pinch cayenne pepper
- 1 ½ tsp olive oil

- 1 egg white
- 4 ounces each tilapia fillets

How to Make

1 Preheat oven to 350 degrees F.
2 In a small baking dish, stir together pecans, breadcrumbs, rosemary, coconut palm sugar, salt and cayenne pepper.
3 Add the olive oil and toss to coat the pecan mixture.
4 Bake until the pecan mixture is light golden brown, 7 to 8 minutes.
5 Increase the heat to 400 degrees F. Coat a large glass baking dish with cooking spray.
6 In a shallow dish, whisk the egg white. Working with one tilapia at a time, dip the fish in the egg white and then the pecan mixture, lightly coating each side.
7 Place the fillets in the prepared baking dish.
8 Press the remaining pecan mixture into the top of the tilapia fillets.
9 Bake until the tilapia is just cooked through, about 10 minutes. Serve. ▨

DAY 19

?

BREAKFAST

Pecan Banana Bread Overnight Oats

Start to End: 20 minutes

Servings: 2

Ingredients

- 1 cup old-fashioned rolled oats
- 1 ½ cups milk
- very ripe bananas, mashed
- ¼ cup plain Greek yogurt
- tbsp. unsweetened coconut flakes, toasted
- 2 tbsp. honey
- 1 tbsp. chia seeds
- 2 tsp. vanilla extract
- 1/4 tsp. flaked sea salt

- Banana slices, roasted pecans, fig halves, honey and pomegranate seeds, for serving

How to Make

- In a medium bowl, stir together the oats; milk; bananas; Greek yogurt; unsweetened coconut flakes; honey; chia seeds; vanilla extract and sea salt until well combined.
- Divide mixture between 2 bowls or glass jars. Cover and refrigerate at least 6 hours or overnight.
- Stir, heat up if desired, and top with banana slices, roasted pecans and fig halves.
- Drizzle with honey and sprinkle with pomegranate seeds.

⁇

LUNCH

Salmon with Greens and Cauliflower Rice

Start to End: 1 hour

Servings: 2

Ingredients

- 2 salmon fillets, sustainably sourced or organic
- 10 to 12 Brussels sprouts, chopped in half
- 1 bunch kale, washed and shredded
- ½ head cauliflower, pulsed into cauliflower rice (you can use a whole cauliflower head if you wish)
- 3 tbsps olive or coconut oil
- 1 tsp curry powder
- Himalayan salt

For Marinade:

- ¼ cup tamari sauce

- 1 tsp Dijon mustard
- 1 tsp sesame oil
- 1 tsp honey or maple syrup (optional)
- 1 tbsp sesame seeds

How to Make

1. Preheat oven to 350°F.
2. Line a baking tray and add chopped Brussels sprouts. Coat with 1 tablespoon oil and season with salt. Add to oven and roast for 20 minutes.
3. Meanwhile, make marinade by combining all ingredients in a bowl and whisking until combined.
4. Remove Brussels sprouts after 20 minutes and add salmon fillets to the baking tray. Spoon marinade over salmon fillets and return to oven for a further 13 to 15 minutes, or until salmon is cooked to your liking.
5. While salmon is cooking, heat a pan over medium-high heat and add 1 tablespoon oil. Add kale and sauté until wilted (2 to 3 minutes). Remove from pan and set aside.
6. Heat remaining oil in pan and add cauliflower rice. Season with 1 teaspoon curry powder and salt and sauté until cooked (2 to 3 minutes).
7. Remove salmon and Brussels sprouts from oven and divide into two bowls. Add sautéed kale and cauliflower rice to bowls.

SNACK

Coconut Lemon Bars

Start to End: 10 minutes

Servings: 12

Ingredients

For the Bar Base:

- Parchment paper or wax paper to line pan
- 1 2/3 cup slivered almonds (blanched) or 1 3/4 cups raw almonds (whole).
- 1 cup raw cashews
- 1 cup unsweetened coconut flakes (to grind)
- 1 tbsp starch (arrowroot or tapioca work best)
- 1/4 cup hot water
- 1/4 cup honey or maple syrup

- Lemon zest
- Optional Lemon juice (1 tbsp)
- 1 tsp vanilla
- Optional lemon extract ½ tsp
- tbsp ground flaxseeds
- All ground then mixed with water/honey and pressed into lined 8×8 pan.

Topping:

- 1/3 cup unsweetened coconut flakes
- Lemon zest/peel
- ½ to 1 tsp coconut oil

How to Make

1   First line an 8×8 pan with parchment paper or wax paper. Set aside.
2   In a food processor or blender, grind your almonds and cashews into a finer mealy texture. I find that slivered almonds (vs whole) work best.
3   Next add in your coconut and blend again until batter is once again, mealy in texture. Pour batter in a large bowl and mix in your starch and 1 tbsp lemon zest.
4   Heat 1/4 cup of water in a heat safe container. Mix your honey, vanilla, and lemon extract or juice into the hot water.
5   Pour the hot water/lemon mixture into the coconut/lemon nut mixture.
6   Mix all together with spoon or hands. Add your ground flaxseed (or protein of choice) last.
7   Press batter into pan, evenly.
8   Finally, make your topping.

Topping and Storage tips:

1. Grind 1/3 cup unsweetened coconut flakes into a finer mixture. You can also just use shredded unsweetened coconut.
2. Mix this with a 3 thinly cut and chopped lemon slices or 1 tbsp lemon zest. and 1/2 to 1 tsp coconut oil.
3. Mix or grind together again. Spread this mixture of the bars. If you are not looking for lower sugar option, feel free to drizzle Optional honey on top.
4. Place pan in fridge for 30 minutes or longer. Once set, remove from fridge and cut into 9-12 s◌uares.
5. Wrap individually and keep in fridge for up to 2 weeks or freezer for up to 6 weeks. ◌

DINNER

Chinese Chicken Salad

Start to End: 35 minutes

Servings: 4

Ingredients

- tbsps low-sodium soy sauce, divided
- tsps toasted sesame oil, divided
- 1 pound skinless, boneless chicken breasts
- ½ head napa cabbage, thinly shredded (about 6 cups)
- ¼ head red cabbage, shredded (about 2 cups)
- 1 large carrot, shredded (about 2 cups)
- scallions, trimmed and thinly sliced, greens included (about 1/2 cup)
- 1 can sliced water chestnuts

- 1 can Mandarin oranges in water, drained
- 1/3 cup rice wine vinegar
- 1 tsp minced garlic
- 1 tsp minced ginger
- tbsps canola oil
- 2 tbsps brown sugar
- 1 ½ tsps chili-garlic sauce or chili sauce
- ¼ cup sliced almonds, toasted

How to Make

1. Preheat oven to 350 degrees F.
2. Combine 1 tablespoon soy sauce and 1/2 teaspoon sesame oil and brush onto chicken breasts.
3. Arrange in a baking dish and bake until juices run clear, about 13 to15 minutes.
4. Remove from oven, cool completely, and cut into 1/4-inch slices.
5. In a large bowl, combine Napa cabbage, red cabbage, carrot, scallions, water chestnuts, Mandarin orange and sliced chicken.
6. In a separate bowl, whisk together 3 tablespoons soy sauce, vinegar, garlic, ginger, oil, 1 1/2 teaspoons sesame oil, brown sugar and chili sauce.
7. Pour dressing over salad and toss to combine.
8. Divide among bowls and top each serving with 2 teaspoons toasted almonds. 🔲

DAY 20

BREAKFAST

Turmeric Latte

Start to End: 5 minutes

Servings: 1

Ingredients

- 1 cup unsweetened almond milk
- ½ tsp turmeric
- 1/3 tsp cinnamon
- dash cayenne pepper
- dash black pepper

Optional:

- 1 teaspoon maple syrup or coconut sugar

- tsps coconut oil

How to Make

1   Place all ingredients in a blender and blend on medium for less than 5 seconds.
2   Pour mix into sauce pan and heat for 2 to 4 minutes over medium heat.
3   Drink and enjoy! ⬚

LUNCH

Broiled Salmon with Spinach

Start to End: 15 minutes

Servings: 1

Ingredients

- ounces fresh wild salmon
- 1 ½ tbsps Dijon mustard
- tbsps low sodium soy sauce or Bragg Liᐧuid Aminos
- 1 cup steamed spinach
- to taste salt
- to taste freshly ground black pepper

How to Make

1 Preheat broiler. Spread the top of the salmon with mustard and drizzle with soy sauce.
2 Place in a baking pan (sprayed with liberally with cooking spray) and broil for 8-10 minutes, or until cooked through.
3 While the salmon is cooking, steam the spinach.
4 Top salmon with spinach and season with salt and pepper to taste. ⏎

SNACK

Coconut Lemon Bars

Start to End: 10 minutes

Servings: 12

Ingredients

For the Bar Base:

- Parchment paper or wax paper to line pan
- 1 2/3 cup slivered almonds (blanched) or 1 3/4 cups raw almonds (whole).
- 1 cup raw cashews
- 1 cup unsweetened coconut flakes (to grind)
- 1 tbsp starch (arrowroot or tapioca work best)
- 1/4 cup hot water
- 1/4 cup honey or maple syrup

- Lemon zest
- Optional Lemon juice (1 tbsp)
- 1 tsp vanilla
- Optional lemon extract ½ tsp
- tbsp ground flaxseeds
- All ground then mixed with water/honey and pressed into lined 8×8 pan.

Topping:

- 1/3 cup unsweetened coconut flakes
- Lemon zest/peel
- ½ to 1 tsp coconut oil

How to Make

1   First line an 8×8 pan with parchment paper or wax paper. Set aside.
2   In a food processor or blender, grind your almonds and cashews into a finer mealy texture. I find that slivered almonds (vs whole) work best.
3   Next add in your coconut and blend again until batter is once again, mealy in texture. Pour batter in a large bowl and mix in your starch and 1 tbsp lemon zest.
4   Heat 1/4 cup of water in a heat safe container. Mix your honey, vanilla, and lemon extract or juice into the hot water.
5   Pour the hot water/lemon mixture into the coconut/lemon nut mixture.
6   Mix all together with spoon or hands. Add your ground flaxseed (or protein of choice) last.
7   Press batter into pan, evenly.
8   Finally, make your topping.

Topping and Storage tips:

1   Grind 1/3 cup unsweetened coconut flakes into a finer mixture. You can also just use shredded unsweetened coconut.

2   Mix this with a 3 thinly cut and chopped lemon slices or 1 tbsp lemon zest. and 1/2 to 1 tsp coconut oil.

3   Mix or grind together again. Spread this mixture of the bars. If you are not looking for lower sugar option, feel free to drizzle Optional honey on top.

4   Place pan in fridge for 30 minutes or longer. Once set, remove from fridge and cut into 9-12 s□uares.

5   Wrap individually and keep in fridge for up to 2 weeks or freezer for up to 6 weeks. □

DINNER

Instant Pot Sweet Potato Curry

Start to End: 50 minutes

Servings: 4

Ingredients

- cups 12-hour soaked, drained, rinsed uncooked chickpeas (1.5 cups dried)
- 1 onion
- cloves garlic
- 1 tbsp avocado oil
- 2-3 tbsp red Thai curry paste
- 1 can coconut milk 400 ml full fat or light
- sweet potatoes
- 100g baby spinach
- sea salt

- sesame seeds
- red chili

How to Make

1   The night before cover 1.5 cups dried chickpeas with abundant water and let soak 12-18 hours. Then drain and rinse well. Set aside.
2   Peel and chop onion and peel and crush garlic.
3   Peel and cube sweet potato.
4   Press "sauté" and wait for the Instant Pot to say "hot". Then add avocado oil, chopped onion and garlic and sauté until translucent.
5   Add red Thai curry paste and coconut milk and stir well until well combined. Season with sea salt if needed (will depend on how salty the curry paste is).
6   Add chickpeas and sweet potato cubes, put on lid and turn valve to sealing position.
7   Set to "manual" high pressure for 18 minutes and let pressure release naturally (will take 15-20 minutes).
8   Once the safety pin drops open the pot and immediately add baby spinach and stir.
9   Serve over brown rice and enjoy or store in meal prep container and store in fridge for 3-4 days or freeze for up to 1 month. ▢

DAY 21

?

BREAKFAST

Turmeric Oatmeal

Start to End: 20 minutes

Servings: 1

Ingredients

Oatmeal:

- ½ cup Whole Rolled Oats
- 1 cup Water
- 1 splash Oat Milk or any other plant milk you like
- ½ tsp Turmeric Powder

Toppings:

- Raspberries
- Blueberries

- Mixed Seeds
- Flaked Almonds
- Dried Cranberries
- Desiccated Coconut
- Mint Leaves
- Maple Syrup (optional)

How to Make

1. Measure the oats, hemp milk, water and spices into a saucepan.
2. Cook over a medium to high heat for about 5 minutes, until it reaches you desired consistency.
3. Top up with raspberries, blueberries, almonds, cranberries and whatever you fancy.

LUNCH

Zucchini Noodles with Roasted Halibut

Start to End: 20 minutes

Servings: 1

Ingredients

- Coconut Oil
- 1 package zucchini noodles (or 3-4 zucchini, spiralized)
- Coconut Aminos
- 1 tbsp red curry paste
- cloves garlic, chopped
- 2-inch piece fresh ginger root, peeled and grated
- scallions, sliced
- ½ cup cilantro, washed and chopped

- ounces wild halibut
- Salt
- ¼ tsp red pepper flakes

How to Make

1 Lightly coat a medium pan with coconut oil and heat over medium-high heat.
2 Add zucchini noodles, curry paste, garlic, and ginger.
3 Cook until noodles are tender, stirring occasionally, about 4 minutes. Season to taste with aminos.
4 Heat another pan lightly coated with coconut oil over medium-high heat. Place fish skin-side down.
5 Season with salt and red pepper flakes.
6 Turn broiler on in oven.
7 Cook for 7 minutes and then transfer to oven. Broil for 5 minutes or until fish is cooked through. (Cook time will depend on thickness of fish).
8 Add scallions and cilantro to noodles and stir to combine.
9 Transfer to a plate, top with fish, and serve. ▨

SNACK

Citrus Vinaigrette

Start to End: 5 minutes

Servings: 1

Ingredients

- 1 small shallot, finely chopped
- ¾ cup olive oil
- ¼ cup Champagne vinegar or white wine vinegar
- 3 tbsps fresh lemon juice
- 2 tbsps fresh orange juice
- ¼ tsp finely grated lemon zest
- Kosher salt and freshly ground black pepper

How to Make

1. Combine the first 6 ingredients in a small jar; season vinaigrette to taste with salt and pepper.
2. Shake to blend. ⏷

DINNER

Salmon and Quinoa Bowls with Kale and Tahini-Yogurt Sauce

Start to End: 30 minutes

Servings: 4

Ingredients

- 1 cup white quinoa
- 1 bunch Lacinato, Tuscan or dinosaur kale, thick stems removed and thinly sliced
- 1 medium carrot, peeled and thinly sliced
- 2 tbsps lemon juice
- garlic cloves, minced

- Olive oil
- Sea salt
- cups cooked chickpeas, rinsed and drained if canned
- 1/4 cup dried currants, cranberries or cherries
- 1 tbsps hemp seeds (optional)
- Four 4-ounce sockeye salmon fillets (skin on)

For the sauce:

- ¼ cup tahini
- ½ cup water
- 1 tbsp lemon juice
- ½ cup Greek yogurt
- ½ tsp sea salt

How to Make

1. In a medium saucepan, combine the quinoa and 2 cups water. Bring to a boil, cover, and reduce the heat to low.
2. Cook for 15 minutes, then let stand covered for 10 minutes off the heat. Fluff with a fork and set aside.
3. Meanwhile in a large mixing bowl, combine the kale, carrots, lemon juice, garlic, 2 tablespoons of olive oil and 1/2 teaspoon sea salt.
4. With clean hands, toss the kale until very well coated in the lemon and oil.
5. Add the cooked quinoa to the kale along with the chickpeas, dried fruit and hemp seeds (if using). Mix until well-incorporated and taste for seasoning.
6. Heat 2 tablespoons of oil in a large nonstick or cast iron skillet. Pat the salmon dry and season with salt.
7. Cook the salmon skin-side down over high heat until nicely browned, 2-3 minutes.

8. Carefully flip the fish and cook for another 2 minutes, until opaque up the sides.
9. Divide the quinoa between 4 bowls and top with the seared salmon.
10. In a medium mixing bowl, whisk together the ingredients for the sauce until smooth.
11. Add more water as necessary to make the sauce drizzle-friendly. Spoon over the fish and serve immediately.

DAY 22

[?]

BREAKFAST

Cinnamon Spice Roasted Pepitas

Start to End: 50 minutes

Servings: 6

Ingredients

- 1 cup raw pepitas
- 1 tsp coconut oil (melted)
- 1 tsp honey (melted)
- 1 tsp cinnamon
- ½ tsp sea salt (optional)

How to Make

1. Preheat oven to 325 degrees.

2. Line a baking sheet with parchment paper.
3. Combine coconut oil, honey, cinnamon, and salt in a mixing bowl and stir to combine.
4. Add pepitas to mixture and toss to evenly coat.
5. Spread the mixture evenly on the baking sheet in a single layer.
6. Bake for 30 minutes - 45 minutes, tossing every 15 minutes until golden brown and crispy. ▢

LUNCH

Strawberry Chia Jam

Start to End: 20 minutes

Servings: 2

Ingredients

- cups fresh strawberries, diced
- 1 tbsp raw honey, as needed for sweetness (use pure maple syrup if vegan)
- 1/4 cup chia seeds, plus more as needed, to thicken

How to Make

1 Add the strawberries to a saucepan and set over medium heat.

2   Cook until the strawberries break down and become liquidly, about 5 to 10 minutes.

3   Mash the fruit with the back of a spatula or a potato masher. You can make it as smooth or as lumpy as you'd like here for the texture of the jam.

4   Remove the pan from the heat, and stir in the honey. Taste, and add more honey, as needed, for additional sweetness. If vegan, use pure maple syrup instead of raw honey.

5   Add the chia seeds, and stir to combine.

6   Let stand 5-10 minutes, or until thickened. The jam will continue to thicken, especially once refrigerated, but if you'd like a thicker consistency, particularly with very high-liquid fruits, you can stir in more chia seeds 1 tablespoon at a time.

7   Once the jam has cooled to room temperature, transfer it to a jar or sealable mason jar. ▢

SNACK

Sweet Potato Toast with Blueberries

Start to End: 15 minutes

Servings: 4

Ingredients

- medium sweet potatoes
- 1 cup cottage cheese
- Fresh strawberries and blueberries

How to Make

1   On a large cutting board, trim the sweet potato ends. Slice the sweet potato lengthwise into 1/4-inch slabs using a large knife, about 4 slices per potato.

2   Place the sweet potatoes in the toaster oven and toast until the potatoes are lightly browned and fork tender in the center.

3   In a regular toaster, toast standing up, for 2 toast cycles.

4   Once sweet potatoes are cooked through and toasted spread cottage cheese over each slice, top with berries and enjoy. ⏹

DINNER

Spiced Lentil Soup

Start to End: 55 minutes

Servings: 4

Ingredients

- ¼ cup extra virgin olive oil
- 1 medium yellow or white onion, chopped
- carrots, peeled and chopped
- 4 garlic cloves, pressed or minced
- 2 tsps ground cumin
- 1 tsp curry powder
- ½ tsp dried thyme
- 1 large can (28 ounces) diced tomatoes, lightly drained

- 1 cup brown or green lentils, picked over and rinsed
- 4 cups vegetable broth
- cups water
- 1 tsp salt, more to taste
- Pinch of red pepper flakes
- Freshly ground black pepper, to taste
- 1 cup chopped fresh collard greens or kale, tough ribs removed
- 1 to 2 tbsps lemon juice (½ to 1 medium lemon), to taste

How to Make

1   Warm the olive oil in a large Dutch oven or pot over medium heat. One-fourth cup olive oil may seem like a lot, but it adds a lovely richness and heartiness to this nutritious soup.
2   Once the oil is shimmering, add the chopped onion and carrot and cook, stirring often, until the onion has softened and is turning translucent, about 5 minutes.
3   Add the garlic, cumin, curry powder and thyme. Cook until fragrant while stirring constantly, about 30 seconds.
4   Pour in the drained diced tomatoes and cook for a few more minutes, stirring often, in order to enhance their flavor.
5   Pour in the lentils, broth and the water. Add 1 teaspoon salt and a pinch of red pepper flakes.
6   Season generously with freshly ground black pepper.
7   Raise heat and bring the mixture to a boil, then partially cover the pot and reduce the heat to maintain a gentle simmer.
8   Cook for 25 to 30 minutes, or until the lentils are tender but still hold their shape.
9   Transfer 2 cups of the soup to a blender. Securely fasten the lid, protect your hand from steam with a tea towel placed over the lid, and purée the soup until smooth.

10 Pour the puréed soup back into the pot. (Or, use an immersion blender to blend a portion of the soup.)

11 Add the chopped greens and cook for 5 more minutes, or until the greens have softened to your liking.

12 Remove the pot from the heat and stir in 1 tablespoon of lemon juice.

13 Taste and season with more salt, pepper and/or lemon juice until the flavors really sing. For spicier soup, add another pinch or two of red pepper flakes.

14 Serve while hot. Leftovers will keep well for about 4 days in the refrigerator, or can be frozen for several months (just defrost before serving). ⬚

DAY 23

?

BREAKFAST

Cherry Coconut Porridge

Start to End: 10 minutes

Servings: 1

Ingredients

- 1.5cups oats
- 4 tbsps chia seed
- 3-4 cups of coconut drinking milk
- 3 tbsps raw cacao
- pinch of stevia
- coconut shavings
- cherries (fresh or frozen)
- dark chocolate shavings
- maple syrup

How to Make

1. Combine oats, chia, coconut milk, cacao and stevia in a saucepan.
2. Bring to a boil over medium heat and then simmer over lower heat until oats are cooked.
3. Pour into a bowl and top with coconut shavings, cherries, dark chocolate shavings and maple syrup to taste. ⏺

LUNCH

Zucchini Noodles with Roasted Halibut

Start to End: 20 minutes

Servings: 1

Ingredients

- Coconut Oil
- 1 package zucchini noodles (or 3-4 zucchini, spiralized)
- Coconut Aminos
- 1 tbsp red curry paste
- cloves garlic, chopped
- 2-inch piece fresh ginger root, peeled and grated
- scallions, sliced
- ½ cup cilantro, washed and chopped

- ounces wild halibut
- Salt
- ¼ tsp red pepper flakes

How to Make

1. Lightly coat a medium pan with coconut oil and heat over medium-high heat.
2. Add zucchini noodles, curry paste, garlic, and ginger.
3. Cook until noodles are tender, stirring occasionally, about 4 minutes. Season to taste with aminos.
4. Heat another pan lightly coated with coconut oil over medium-high heat. Place fish skin-side down.
5. Season with salt and red pepper flakes.
6. Turn broiler on in oven.
7. Cook for 7 minutes and then transfer to oven. Broil for 5 minutes or until fish is cooked through. (Cook time will depend on thickness of fish).
8. Add scallions and cilantro to noodles and stir to combine.
9. Transfer to a plate, top with fish, and serve. ⍰

⍰

SNACK

Power Balls

Start to End: 45 minutes

Servings: 25

Ingredients

- ½ Cup puffed millet
- 1 cup puffed kamut or puffed rice
- ½ cup diced dried plums
- 1/3 cup semisweet chocolate chips
- ¼ cup sesame seeds
- 1/3 cup sunflower butter, at room temperature
- ½ cup honey
- ¾ cup shredded unsweetened coconut

How to Make

1. In a large bowl, toss together the puffed millet and puffed kamut or rice.
2. Add the dried plums, chocolate chips, and sesame seeds.
3. Stir in the sunflower butter and the honey. You should have a nice sticky mess!
4. Cover the bowl with plastic wrap and refrigerate for 30 minutes.
5. Place the coconut in a small bowl. Using a tablespoon, scoop the mixture and form it into 1-inch (2.5cm) balls with your hands.
6. Roll the balls in the coconut and transfer to a container.
7. You can store the power balls in the refrigerator for up to 1 week, or in the freezer in a zip-top freezer bag for up to 1 month, but I bet they won't last that long!

DINNER

Polenta with Wild Mushroom Bolognese

Start to End: 35 minutes

Servings: 4

Ingredients

- ounces white mushrooms, stems removed
- tablespoons olive oil, divided
- 1 ½ cups finely chopped onion
- ½ cup finely chopped carrot (about 1 medium carrot)
- 4 garlic cloves, minced
- 1 (18-ounce) tube plain polenta, cut into 8 slices
- ¼ cup tomato paste
- 1 tbsp dried oregano, crushed between your fingers
- 1/4 tsp ground nutmeg

- 1/4 tsp salt
- ¼ tsp freshly ground pepper
- ½ cup dry red wine
- 3/4 cup soy milk
- 1/2 tsp sugar

How to Make

1 Place half of the mushrooms in a food processor bowl and pulse about 15 times until finely chopped but not pureed, similar to the texture of ground meat. Repeat with the remaining mushrooms and set aside. (To save time, you can also use the food processor to chop the onion, carrot and garlic!)

2 In a large stockpot over medium-high heat, heat 2 tablespoons of oil. Add the onion and carrot and cook for 5 minutes, stirring occasionally. Add the mushrooms and garlic and cook for 5 minutes, stirring fre uently.

3 While the vegetables are cooking, add the remaining 1 tablespoon oil in a large skillet and heat over medium-high heat.

4 Add 4 slices of polenta to the skillet and cook for 3-4 minutes, until golden; flip and cook for 3-4 minutes more. Remove polenta from the skillet, place it on a shallow serving dish and cover with aluminum foil to keep warm. Repeat with remaining 4 slices of polenta.

5 To the mushroom mixture, add the tomato paste, oregano, nutmeg, salt, pepper and stir.

6 Continue cooking for another 2-3 minutes, until the vegetables have softened and begin to brown. Add the wine and cook for 1-2 minutes, scraping up any bits from the bottom of the pan while stirring with a wooden spoon.

7   Cook until the wine is nearly all evaporated. Lower the heat to medium.

8   Meanwhile, in a small, microwave-safe bowl, mix the milk and sugar together and microwave on high for 30-45 seconds, until hot.

9   Slowly stir the milk into the mushroom mixture and simmer for 4 more minutes, until the milk is absorbed. To serve, pour the mushroom veggie sauce over warm polenta slices. ⬜

DAY 24

?

BREAKFAST

Oat Porridge with Berries

Start to End: 30 minutes

Servings: 4

Ingredients

For The Oats:

- 1 cup steel cut oats
- 3 cups water
- pinch of salt

Toppings:

- fresh or frozen fruit/berries
- a handful of sliced almonds, pepitas, hemp seeds, or other nut/seed

- unsweetened kefir, homemade
- drizzle of maple syrup, sprinkling of coconut sugar, a few drops of stevia, or any other sweetener

How to Make

1 Add the oats to a small saucepan and place over medium-high heat. Allow to toast, stirring or shaking the pan fre?uently, for 2-3 minutes.
2 Add the water and bring to a boil. Reduce the heat to a simmer, and let cook for about 25 minutes, or until the oats are tender enough for your liking. (The oats will thicken up as they cool -- if you prefer them a bit more porridge, add a splash more water, or some milk or dairy-free alternative.)
3 Serve with berries, nuts/seeds (or a handful of granola), a splash of kefir, and any sweetener you like, to taste. ?

?

LUNCH

Dukkah Roasted Vegetables Salad

Start to End: 30 minutes

Servings: 3

Ingredients

- cups chopped cauliflower
- cups sliced or chopped white button mushrooms
- 1 cup sliced peeled pearl onions or 1 shallot
- 1 cup grape tomatoes
- 1/4 c olive or avocado Oil
- 1 tbsp or more dukkah
- 1 tsp minced garlic minced or 1/2 tsp garlic powder
- 1 cup chopped mixed greens (spinach, kale, or shredded brussel sprouts)
- 1/4 c raw pumpkin seeds (pepitas)

- pinch of black pepper
- pinch of sea salt
- tsp lemon juice
- 2 mint leaves (chopped, to garnish) – optional
- 1 sprig of oregano leaves, to garnish
- sliced lemon to garnish
- Micro-greens or sprouts to garnish
- Optional crumbled feta or parmesan to serve (omit for paleo/vegan)
- Optional dried fruit to garnish.
- optional creamy dressing of choice

How to Make

1. Preheat oven to 425F. Line a large sheet pan with parchment paper or grease. Set aside.
2. In large bowl, place all your diced/chopped cauliflower, mushroom, tomatoes, and onions.
3. Toss in 1/4 cup oil and then add in your dukkah spice mix, garlic, salt, pepper, and toss again.
4. Mix in your chopped greens and toss again. Feel free to add in any more vegetables if you'd like more bulk to the salad.
5. Lay the chopped vegetables on the baking sheet and sprinkle the pumpkin seeds on top.
6. Season with salt, pepper, and fresh lemon juice.
7. Roast in oven for 15-20 minutes, checking at 15 minutes for doneness.
8. Once cauliflower is golden brown, remove from oven and toss in pan.
9. Garnish with just a touch fresh mint leaf (optional), lemon slices, and a few leafs of fresh oregano.

10 Serve onto plates with extra green or sprouts. You can also just place in large serving bowl.

11 Drizzle with extra olive oil if needed. Or use your favorite creamy dressing. I love using my warm onion dressing.

12 If you want to make this salad more filling, add in a few tablespoons of chopped dried fruit and crumbled feta. ▢

SNACK

Matcha Smoothie Bowl

Start to End: 5 minutes

Servings: 2

Ingredients

Smoothie:

- 2 peeled, sliced and frozen ripe bananas
- ¼ cup chopped ripe pineapple
- ¾ - 1 cup light coconut milk
- 2 tsp matcha green tea powder
- 1 heaping cup organic spinach or kale

Toppings (optional):

- Fresh berries
- Coconut flake

- Banana slices
- Chia Seeds
- Slivered roasted almonds

How to Make

1. Add frozen banana slices, pineapple (optional), lesser amount of coconut milk, matcha powder, and spinach to a blender and blend on high until creamy and smooth.
2. Add only as much coconut milk as you need to help it blend.
3. Taste and adjust flavor as needed, adding more banana (or a touch of maple syrup or stevia) for sweetness, matcha for more intense green tea flavor, or coconut milk for creaminess. Pineapple will add a little tart/tang, so add more if desired.
4. Divide between two serving bowls and top with desired toppings (optional). Bananas would make a delicious garnish as well.
5. Best when fresh, though leftovers keep well sealed in the refrigerator up to 24 hours. ⬚ ⬚

DINNER

Slow Cooker Turkey Chili

Start to End: 4 hours 20 minutes

Servings: 8

Ingredients

- 1 tablespoon olive oil
- 1 lb 99% lean ground turkey
- 1 medium onion diced
- 1 red pepper chopped
- 1 yellow pepper chopped
- 2 (15 oz) cans tomato sauce
- 2 (15 oz) cans petite diced tomatoes
- 2 (15 oz) cans black beans, rinsed and drained

- 2 (15 oz) cans red kidney beans, rinsed and drained
- 1 (16 oz) jar deli-sliced tamed jalapeno peppers, drained
- 1 cup frozen corn
- tablespoons chili powder
- 1 tablespoon cumin
- Salt and black pepper to taste

Optional Toppings:

- green onions shredded cheese
- avocado
- sour cream/Greek yogurt

How to Make

1. Heat the oil in a skillet over medium heat. Place turkey in the skillet, and cook until brown. Pour turkey into slow cooker.
2. Add the onion, peppers, tomato sauce, diced tomatoes, beans, jalapeños, corn, chili powder, and cumin. Stir and season with salt and pepper.
3. Cover and cook on High for 4 hours or low for 6 hours. Serve with toppings, if desired.
4. Make use of a 6 quart slow cooker. ⬚

DAY 25

?

BREAKFAST

Coffee and Mint Parfait

Start to End: 5 minutes

Servings: 1

Ingredients

- ½ cup plain yogurt
- 2 tsps brewed coffee
- 3-4 drops peppermint Stevia (optional)
- ¼ cup chopped pecans
- coffee granules and fresh mint

How to Make

1 Combine the yogurt, coffee, and stevia (if using) in a small bowl.
2 In a small glass, layer the yogurt with the pecans, alternating until you get to the top.

3   Garnish with coffee granules and fresh mint. ⏲

LUNCH

Cranberry Walnut Salad

Start to End: 8 minutes

Servings: 6

Ingredients

- 2 tbsps olive oil
- 1 tbsp cider vinegar
- ½ tsp agave or honey
- 1 package mesclun greens
- 1 large head frisee, trimmed and torn into bite-size pieces
- 2 tbsps unsweetened, dried cranberries
- 2 tbsps raw walnut pieces

- 1 apple, sliced

How to Make

1 In a medium bowl, whisk together oil, vinegar, and agave or honey. Add mesclun greens and frisee. Toss to coat.
2 Top with cranberries and walnuts. Season with salt and pepper, if desired. ▨

SNACK

Sweet Potato Toast with Blueberries

Start to End: 15 minutes

Servings: 4

Ingredients

- medium sweet potatoes
- 1 cup cottage cheese
- Fresh strawberries and blueberries

How to Make

1   On a large cutting board, trim the sweet potato ends. Slice the sweet potato lengthwise into 1/4-inch slabs using a large knife, about 4 slices per potato.

2　Place the sweet potatoes in the toaster oven and toast until the potatoes are lightly browned and fork tender in the center.
3　In a regular toaster, toast standing up, for 2 toast cycles.
4　Once sweet potatoes are cooked through and toasted spread cottage cheese over each slice, top with berries and enjoy. ⍰

⍰

DINNER

Curried Potatoes with Poached Eggs

Start to End: 40 minutes

Servings: 4

Ingredients

- russet potatoes
- 1 inch fresh ginger
- cloves garlic
- 1 tbsp olive oil
- tbsp curry powder (hot or mild)
- oz can tomato sauce
- large eggs
- 1/2 bunch fresh cilantro (optional)

How to Make

1   Wash the potatoes well, then cut into 3/4-inch cubes. Place the cubed potatoes in a large pot and cover with water. Cover the pot with a lid and bring it up to a boil over high heat.

2   Boil the potatoes for 5-6 minutes, or until they're tender when pierced with a fork. Drain the cooked potatoes in a colander.

3   While the potatoes are boiling, begin the sauce. Peel the ginger with a vegetable peeler or scrape the skin off with the side of a spoon.

4   Use a small holed cheese grater to grate about one inch of ginger (less if you prefer a more subtle ginger flavor). Mince the garlic.

5   Add the ginger, garlic, and olive oil to a large, deep skillet (or a wide based pot).

6   Sauté the ginger and garlic over medium low heat for 1-2 minutes, or just until soft and fragrant. Add the curry powder to the skillet and sauté for about a minute more to toast the spices.

7   Add the tomato sauce to the skillet and stir to combine. Turn the heat up to medium and heat the sauce through. Taste the sauce and add salt, if needed. Add the cooked and drained potatoes to the skillet and stir to coat in the sauce. Add a couple tablespoons of water if the mixture seems dry or pasty.

8   Create four small wells or dips in the potato mixture and crack an egg into each. Place a lid on the skillet and let it come up to a simmer.

9   Simmer the eggs in the sauce for 6-10 minutes, or until cooked through (less time if runny yolks are desired). Top with chopped fresh cilantro. ▢

DAY 26

?

BREAKFAST

Turmeric Oatmeal

Start to End: 20 minutes

Servings: 1

Ingredients

Oatmeal:

- ½ cup Whole Rolled Oats
- 1 cup Water
- 1 splash Oat Milk or any other plant milk you like
- ½ tsp Turmeric Powder

Toppings:

- Raspberries
- Blueberries

- Mixed Seeds
- Flaked Almonds
- Dried Cranberries
- Desiccated Coconut
- Mint Leaves
- Maple Syrup (optional)

How to Make

1. Measure the oats, hemp milk, water and spices into a saucepan.
2. Cook over a medium to high heat for about 5 minutes, until it reaches you desired consistency.
3. Top up with raspberries, blueberries, almonds, cranberries and whatever you fancy.

LUNCH

Lettuce Wraps with Smoked Trout

Start to End: 40 minutes

Servings: 4

Ingredients

- 2 medium carrots, peeled
- 1/2 unpeeled English hothouse cucumber (do not remove seeds)
- 1/4 cup thinly sliced shallots
- 1/4 cup thinly sliced jalapeño chiles with seeds (preferably red; about 2 large)
- 2 tbsps fresh lime juice or unseasoned rice vinegar
- 1 tbsp sugar
- 1 tbsp fish sauce

- 4.5-ounce packages skinless smoked trout fillets, broken into bite-size pieces (about 2 cups)
- 1 cup diced grape tomatoes
- 1/2 cup whole fresh mint leaves
- 1/2 cup small whole fresh basil leaves
- 16 small to medium inner leaves of romaine lettuce (from about 2 hearts of romaine)
- 1/3 cup (about) Asian sweet chili sauce
- 1/4 cup finely chopped lightly salted dry-roasted peanuts

How to Make

1 Using vegetable peeler, shave carrots and cucumber lengthwise into ribbons.

2 Cut ribbons into 3-inch-long sections, then cut sections into matchstick-size strips.

3 Place in large bowl. Add shallots, jalapeños, lime juice, sugar, and fish sauce; let marinate 30 minutes at room temperature.

4 Add trout pieces and tomatoes to vegetable mixture and toss to blend.

5 Transfer trout-vegetable mixture to large strainer and drain off liquid. Return trout-vegetable mixture to same bowl; add mint and basil and toss to blend.

6 Arrange lettuce leaves on large platter. Divide trout-vegetable salad among lettuce leaves. Drizzle sweet chili sauce over each salad and sprinkle with peanuts. ⁂

SNACK

Coconut Lemon Bars

Start to End: 10 minutes

Servings: 12

Ingredients

For the Bar Base:

- Parchment paper or wax paper to line pan
- 1 2/3 cup slivered almonds (blanched) or 1 3/4 cups raw almonds (whole).
- 1 cup raw cashews
- 1 cup unsweetened coconut flakes (to grind)
- 1 tbsp starch (arrowroot or tapioca work best)
- 1/4 cup hot water
- 1/4 cup honey or maple syrup

- Lemon zest
- Optional Lemon juice (1 tbsp)
- 1 tsp vanilla
- Optional lemon extract ½ tsp
- tbsp ground flaxseeds
- All ground then mixed with water/honey and pressed into lined 8×8 pan.

Topping:

- 1/3 cup unsweetened coconut flakes
- Lemon zest/peel
- ½ to 1 tsp coconut oil

How to Make

1. First line an 8×8 pan with parchment paper or wax paper. Set aside.
2. In a food processor or blender, grind your almonds and cashews into a finer mealy texture. I find that slivered almonds (vs whole) work best.
3. Next add in your coconut and blend again until batter is once again, mealy in texture. Pour batter in a large bowl and mix in your starch and 1 tbsp lemon zest.
4. Heat 1/4 cup of water in a heat safe container. Mix your honey, vanilla, and lemon extract or juice into the hot water.
5. Pour the hot water/lemon mixture into the coconut/lemon nut mixture.
6. Mix all together with spoon or hands. Add your ground flaxseed (or protein of choice) last.
7. Press batter into pan, evenly.
8. Finally, make your topping.

Topping and Storage tips:

1   Grind 1/3 cup unsweetened coconut flakes into a finer mixture. You can also just use shredded unsweetened coconut.
2   Mix this with a 3 thinly cut and chopped lemon slices or 1 tbsp lemon zest. and 1/2 to 1 tsp coconut oil.
3   Mix or grind together again. Spread this mixture of the bars. If you are not looking for lower sugar option, feel free to drizzle Optional honey on top.
4   Place pan in fridge for 30 minutes or longer. Once set, remove from fridge and cut into 9-12 squares.
5   Wrap individually and keep in fridge for up to 2 weeks or freezer for up to 6 weeks.

DINNER

Salmon with Greens and Cauliflower Rice

Start to End: 1 hour

Servings: 2

Ingredients

- 2 salmon fillets, sustainably sourced or organic
- 10 to 12 Brussels sprouts, chopped in half
- 1 bunch kale, washed and shredded
- ½ head cauliflower, pulsed into cauliflower rice (you can use a whole cauliflower head if you wish)
- 3 tbsps olive or coconut oil
- 1 tsp curry powder
- Himalayan salt

For Marinade:

- ¼ cup tamari sauce

- 1 tsp Dijon mustard
- 1 tsp sesame oil
- 1 tsp honey or maple syrup (optional)
- 1 tbsp sesame seeds

How to Make

1. Preheat oven to 350°F.
2. Line a baking tray and add chopped Brussels sprouts. Coat with 1 tablespoon oil and season with salt. Add to oven and roast for 20 minutes.
3. Meanwhile, make marinade by combining all ingredients in a bowl and whisking until combined.
4. Remove Brussels sprouts after 20 minutes and add salmon fillets to the baking tray. Spoon marinade over salmon fillets and return to oven for a further 13 to 15 minutes, or until salmon is cooked to your liking.
5. While salmon is cooking, heat a pan over medium-high heat and add 1 tablespoon oil. Add kale and sauté until wilted (2 to 3 minutes). Remove from pan and set aside.
6. Heat remaining oil in pan and add cauliflower rice. Season with 1 teaspoon curry powder and salt and sauté until cooked (2 to 3 minutes).
7. Remove salmon and Brussels sprouts from oven and divide into two bowls. Add sautéed kale and cauliflower rice to bowls. �

DAY 27

?

BREAKFAST

Golden Milk

Start to End: 5 minutes

Servings: 5

Ingredients

- 1 ½ cups light coconut milk (canned is best, but carton works too)
- 1 ½ cups unsweetened plain almond milk (DIY or store-bought)
- 1 ½ tsp ground turmeric
- ¼ tsp ground ginger
- 1 whole cinnamon stick

- 1 tbsp coconut oil
- 1 pinch ground black pepper
- Sweetener of choice (i.e. maple syrup, coconut sugar, or stevia to taste)

How to Make

1 To a small saucepan, add coconut milk, almond milk, ground turmeric, ground ginger, cinnamon stick, coconut oil, black pepper, and sweetener of choice

2 Whisk to combine and warm over medium heat. Heat until hot to the touch but not boiling - about 4 minutes - whisking frequently.

3 Turn off heat and taste to adjust flavor. Add more sweetener to taste or more turmeric or ginger for intense spice + flavor.

4 Serve immediately, dividing between two glasses and leaving the cinnamon stick behind. Best when fresh, though leftovers can be stored covered in the refrigerator for 2-3 days. Reheat on the stovetop or microwave until hot.

LUNCH

Thai Pumpkin Soup

Start to End: 1 hour

Servings: 4

Ingredients

- 1 tbsp vegetable oil
- 1 brown onion, chopped
- 1.2kg kent pumpkin, peeled, chopped
- 300g cream delight potatoes, peeled, chopped
- 2 garlic cloves, crushed
- ¼ cup Thai red curry paste
- ½ cups Massel chicken style liꝗuid stock
- 400ml can coconut milk
- 2 tbsps unsalted roasted peanuts, finely chopped

- 2 tbsps fresh coriander leaves, chopped
- 1 green onion, finely chopped
- 2 tsps lime juice

How to Make

1 Heat oil in a large saucepan over medium-high heat. Cook onion, stirring occasionally, for 5 minutes or until softened. Add pumpkin and potato. Cook, stirring for 5 minutes. Add garlic. Cook, stirring for 1 minute or until fragrant.

2 Add curry paste to pan. Cook, stirring for 2 minutes, to coat vegetables all over. Add stock, stirring to combine. Cover.

3 Bring to the boil. Reduce heat to low. Simmer for 15 minutes. Remove lid. Simmer for a further 15 to 20 minutes or until vegetables are tender.

4 Remove from heat. Stand for 5 minutes.

5 Using a stick blender, blend soup until smooth.

6 Return to medium heat. Stir in 1 cup coconut milk. Season with pepper. Cook, stirring occasionally, for 5 to 6 minutes or until heated through.

7 Meanwhile, combine peanuts, coriander, green onion and lime juice in a small bowl. Ladle soup into bowls. Serve drizzled with remaining coconut milk and sprinkled with peanut mixture. ⬜

SNACK

Lemon Turmeric Energy Balls

Start to End: 10 minutes

Servings: 24

Ingredients

- 12 Medjool dates
- 1 cup rolled oats gluten free
- ½ cup almonds
- 1 tbsp chia seeds
- tbsps lemon juice
- 1 tsp lemon zest
- 1 tsp vanilla extract
- 1 tsp turmeric powder
- Pinch of black pepper
- ½ cup shredded coconut for dusting

How to Make

1 Remove the pits from dates and soak them in hot water for several minutes.
2 When the dates are softened, drain them and place in food processor. Save the water.
3 Add the other ingredients to a food processor and blend until mixture turns into a dough-like consistency.
4 Add 1 tablespoon of water in which you have soaked the dates if the mixture is too dry.
5 With the small spoon scoop the mixture and roll into balls. Roll the balls in shredded coconut and place on the baking sheet.
6 Store energy balls in an airtight container in the refrigerator until serving. ⏹

DINNER

One Pan Lemon Sage Baked Chicken and Olives

Start to End: 30 minutes

Servings: 4

Ingredients

For the Lemon Sage Sauce (Marinade):

- 1 to 2 tbsp chopped sage
- 1 tsp grated lemon
- 2 tbsp lemon juice
- 1 tsp minced garlic- 2 cloves
- 1 tsp onion powder or 1/4 c chopped yellow onion
- 1/4 to 1/3 c olive oil. If you are using fresh onion, use the 1/3 c oil to blend more evenly

- 1/4 tsp kosher salt or fine sea salt
- Crushed black pepper to taste
- 1/4 tsp paprika – optional for kick of spice
- 1 tbsp dijon mustard or honey mustard

For the Pan:

- 1 ½ lbs or 16-17 ounces skinless chicken thighs (see notes if using chicken breast)
- 1 to 2 ounces green olives
- Handful of sliced onion
- Lemon slices to place on chicken
- Black pepper to season on top
- Extra Sage leaves to garnish

Optional

- Vegetable boost –1 cup chopped vegetable of choice.
- Toss in 1 tsp oil, pinch of salt/pepper and add to the pan or on separate pan to bake/roast with chicken.

How to Make

1. Preheat Oven to 400F.
2. First blend your lemon sage marinade. Blend marinade ingredients all together in food processor or blender until a creamy yellow sauce is formed.
3. Place cleaned/trimmed skinless chicken in large bowl or casserole dish.
4. Pour the marinade over the chicken thighs or chicken breast. Place chicken in fridge to marinate 10 to 20 minutes. This is optional but gives it more flavor. If you are using chicken breast, you might want to marinade for 15 to 25 minutes in fridge first.

5. Next place all the marinated chicken in an oven safe skillet or keep in a large casserole dish.
6. Add your olives and onion slices around the chicken and lemon slices on top of each chicken.
7. Season with extra salt/pepper.
8. Bake/Roast for 20-25 minutes, checking internal temperature at 20 minutes to see progress. If you are using thick chicken breast, you might have to bake longer.
9. Broil last 2-3 minutes to create a crispy outside on the chicken and lemon slices on top.
10. Remove and let cool for a few minutes before touching chicken after broiling.
11. Serve baked chicken with the marinade and garnish with sage leaves. ⬜

Day 28

?

BREAKFAST

5-Minute Herb Baked Eggs

Start to End: 10 minutes

Servings: 1

Ingredients

- 1 teaspoon melted butter
- 1 tablespoon milk
- 2 eggs
- Sprinkle of garlic powder, dried thyme, dried oregano, dried parsley, and dried dill

How to Make

1   Set your oven to "Broil" mode, on low.

2   Coat the bottom of a small baking dish with the butter and milk.

3   Crack the eggs on top of butter and milk combination (or crack in a separate bowl, and pour on top). Sprinkle with garlic and dried herbs.

4   Bake for 5-6 minutes, until the eggs are cooked to your liking. ⏹

LUNCH

Tomato Basil Garlic Chicken

Start to End: 20 minutes

Servings: 4

Ingredients

- 4 chicken breasts fillets, skinless and boneless*
- Salt and pepper, to season
- 1/2 teaspoon garlic powder
- 1 tbsp butter, divided
- 1 tbsp olive oil, divided
- 2 cups grape tomatoes, halved
- 1/4 cup fresh basil, shredded
- 1 ½ tbsps minced garlic or 6 large cloves of garlic

How to Make

1   Lightly pound chicken breasts between 2 sheets of parchment paper until they are all the same thickness. Season with salt, pepper and garlic powder.
2   Heat 2 teaspoons of oil and 2 teaspoons of butter in a skillet or pan over medium-high heat.
3   Fry breasts on both sides until golden browned and completely cooked through (about 5-6 minutes per side, depending on the thickness of your fillets).
4   Once cooked, transfer to a plate and tent with foil to keep warm.
5   Heat remaining butter and oil in the pan. Fry garlic until fragrant (about one minute). Add the tomatoes and cook for two minutes, or until they just begin to soften. Turn off the heat and stir through basil.
6   Season with any extra salt and pepper, if needed. Add the chicken back into the pan, and spoon the pan juices and tomato/garlic mixture all over the chicken!
7   Perfect to serve with a salad, garlic bread, rice or pasta!
8   Serve with balsamic glaze for extra flavour! ⏺

SNACK

Citrus Vinaigrette

Start to End: 5 minutes

Servings: 1

Ingredients

- 1 small shallot, finely chopped
- ¾ cup olive oil
- ¼ cup Champagne vinegar or white wine vinegar
- 3 tbsps fresh lemon juice
- 2 tbsps fresh orange juice
- ¼ tsp finely grated lemon zest
- Kosher salt and freshly ground black pepper

How to Make

1   Combine the first 6 ingredients in a small jar; season
    vinaigrette to taste with salt and pepper.
2   Shake to blend. ▨

DINNER

Baked Turkey Meatballs

Start to End: 40 minutes

Servings: 25

Ingredients

- 1 pound ground turkey
- ½ cup fresh breadcrumbs, white or whole wheat
- ½ cup fresh grated Parmesan cheese
- 1 tbsp chopped fresh parsley
- ½ tbsp chopped fresh basil
- ½ tbsp chopped fresh oregano
- 1 large egg, beaten
- Pinch fresh grated nutmeg
- 2-3 tablespoons milk (or water)

How to Make

1   Preheat your oven to 350 degrees.
2   Line two baking sheets with parchment paper.
3   Combine the turkey, breadcrumbs, cheese, herbs, egg, nutmeg, salt and pepper, and milk in a large bowl. You may need to adjust the amount of milk you use based on how dry your bread is, etc. The mixture should be wet enough to stick together, but not loose.
4   Using a teaspoon (for uniformity) or your hands, roll portions of the meat into approximately 1-inch balls, and drop them onto a baking sheet. You should end up with 25-30 meatballs.
5   Bake the meatballs for approximately 30 minutes, turning once, so that the meat is cooked through and all sides are lightly browned. ⏎

DAY 29

?

BREAKFAST

Ancient Grains Breakfast Bowl

Start to End: 30 minutes

Servings: 2

Ingredients

- 1 cup of grains such as amaranth, buckwheat, or ꝗuinoa
- 2½ cups coconut water or nut milk
- 1 cinnamon stick
- 2 whole cloves
- 1 star anise pod (optional)
- Fresh Fruit: apples, pears, blackberries, cranberries, persimmons, etc.
- Maple syrup (optional)

How to Make

1 Place the grains, coconut water/nut milk, and spices in a saucepan and bring to a boil.
2 Once boiling, cover and reduce the heat the medium-low.
3 Cook for approximately 20-25 minutes until the grains are tender.
4 Remove from the heat and discard the whole spices.
5 Serve with desired fruit and a drizzle of maple syrup, if desired. ⏲

LUNCH

Kale Caesar Salad with Grilled Chicken Wrap

Start to End: 10 minutes

Servings: 2

- Ingredients
- 8 ounces grilled chicken, thinly sliced
- 6 cups curly kale, cut into bite sized pieces
- 1 cup cherry tomatoes, quartered
- 3/4 cup finely shredded Parmesan cheese
- ½ coddled egg (cooked about 1 minute)
- 1 clove garlic, minced
- 1/2 tsp Dijon mustard
- 1 teaspoon honey or agave

- 1/8 cup fresh lemon juice
- 1/8 cup olive oil
- Kosher salt and freshly ground black pepper
- 2 Lavash flat breads or two large tortillas

How to Make

1   In a bowl, mix together the half of a coddled egg, minced garlic, mustard, honey, lemon juice and olive oil. Whisk until you have formed a dressing. Season to taste with salt and pepper.

2   Add the kale, chicken and cherry tomatoes and toss to coat with the dressing and ¼ cup of the shredded parmesan.

3   Spread out the two lavash flatbreads. Evenly distribute the salad over the two wraps and sprinkle each with ¼ cup of parmesan.

4   Roll up the wraps and slice in half. Eat immediately

SNACK

Rosemary-Tangerine Cooler

Start to End: 10 minutes

Servings: 2

Ingredients

- 2 tbsps raw sugar plus more
- 2 tangerines, halved crosswise
- 16 rosemary sprigs, divided
- 2 cups white rum

How to Make

1   Heat a cast-iron skillet or griddle over high heat, or on a grill grate. Pour some raw sugar into a small plate. Dip cut sides of tangerines into sugar.
2   Scatter 8 rosemary sprigs in skillet; add tangerines, cut side down.

3   Cook until sugar caramelizes, about 2 minutes. Let cool.
4   Quarter tangerines; discard rosemary. Place tangerines in a
     pitcher, add 2 tbsp. raw sugar, and muddle to release juices.
     Add rum and 6 cups ice; stir until pitcher is frosty.
5   Divide among glasses; garnish with remaining 8 rosemary
     sprigs. ▢

DINNER

Crockpot Bean Bolognese

Start to End: 6 hours 20 minutes

Servings: 4

Ingredients

- 1 medium-size onion, chopped
- 2 carrots, peeled and chopped
- 2 celery stalks, chopped
- 2 cloves garlic, minced
- 1 14-ounce can white beans (such as Cannellini, Great Northern, or Navy)
- 1 28-ounce can crushed tomatoes
- Pasta (optional)

How to Make

1 Place all ingredients in a crock pot set on low.
2 Cook for approximately 4-6 hours until all ingredients are tender.
3 Serve as a chunky stew (add a ½ cup water to the mix if you prefer a looser consistency!) or as a sauce on top of cooked pasta. ⏺

DAY 30

?

BREAKFAST

Coconut Flour Pancakes

Start to End: 20 minutes

Servings: 5

Ingredients

- 2 eggs and 1 extra egg white
- 1/3 cup of almond milk or coconut drinking milk
- 1/4 cup coconut flour -sifted
- 1 tbsp ground flaxseed
- 1 very ripe small banana or half a large banana
- 1 tsp vanilla extract
- 1 tsp ⍰uality apple cider vinegar or distilled vinegar
- ½ teaspoon baking powder
- 1/8 tsp salt
- 1/8 tsp cinnamon optional

- Optional sweetener of choice

How to Make

1 First place egg and milk in a blender or bowl to mix/beat. If you're making the banana version, blend the banana in with the eggs and milk first.
2 Mix in the the coconut flour (a little at a time, whisking) with the egg/milk mix until smooth and not clumpy.
3 Gently stir in the remaining ingredients and beat/blend again until smooth batter is formed. Place in fridge to set for 10-15 minutes.
4 Remove from fridge once batter has set.
5 Heat a skillet to medium high, adding a few teaspoons of oil to coat the pan.
6 Once hot, scoop 1/4 cup batter and pour into the center of the pan. Pancakes flip better with thinner batter (See notes). Also, a crepe pan or non stick griddle for pancakes works best!
7 Cook until the edges start to brown or the middle starts to bubble, which is usually no more than 2 -3 minutes.
8 Flip over and let pancake cook another 1-3 minutes. See notes for cooking times.
9 Remove pancake and place on plate. Repeat to get 3-6 pancakes. The banana sweetened coconut flour pancakes will produce more. All 5-6 inches wide.
10 Top pancakes with extra berries, nuts, and, butter, optional maple syrup.

LUNCH

Quinoa and Citrus Salad

Start to End: 10 minutes

Servings: 1

Ingredients

- 1 cup cooked quinoa, cooled
- 2 small oranges, supremed
- 1 celery rib, finely chopped
- 20g Brazil nuts, chopped
- 1 green onion, sliced
- ¼ cup fresh parsley, finely chopped

For the Dressing:

- juice from above oranges

- ½ tsp lemon juice
- ½ tsp fresh ginger, grated
- 1 tsp white wine vinegar
- 1 small clove garlic, minced
- ½ tsp salt
- ¼ tsp black pepper
- pinch cinnamon

How to Make

1. Cut the oranges into supremes, working over a bowl, in order not lose any of the juice.
2. When you've got all your supremes done, make sure to squeeze all the juice out of the "membranes" that are left behind.
3. Transfer that juice to your mini blender or food processor.
4. Add the rest of the ingredients for the dressing and blend until smooth.
5. Cut your orange supremes into bite size pieces and add them to a medium size mixing bowl. Add the rest of the ingredients, including the dressing, and stir until well combined.
6. Serve immediately, or keep in the refrigerator until ready to serve.

SNACK

Apple Chips

Start to End: 1 hour 30 minutes

Servings: 6

Ingredients

4	Golden Delicious apples, cored and thinly sliced
3	1 ½ tsps white sugar
4	½ tsp ground cinnamon

How to Make

1 Preheat oven to 225 degrees F (110 degrees C).
2 Arrange apples slices on a metal baking sheet.
3 Mix sugar and cinnamon together in a bowl; sprinkle over apple slices.

4   Bake in the preheated until apples are dried and edges curl up, 45 minutes to 1 hour.

5   Transfer apple chips, using a metal spatula, to a wire rack until cooled and crispy. ⬚

DINNER

One-Pan Roasted Chicken with Turmeric

Start to End: 1 hour

Servings: 6

Ingredients

- 1/2 cup extra virgin olive oil
- 1/2 cup dry white wine
- 1/2 cup orange juice
- 1 lime, juice of
- 2 tbsp yellow mustard
- 3 tbsp brown sugar, more for later
- 1 tbsp garlic powder
- 3/4 tbsp ground turmeric spice
- 1 tsp ground corriander
- 1 tsp sweet paprika

- Salt and Pepper
- 1 large fennel bulb, cored, sliced
- 1 large sweet onion, sliced into half moons
- 6 pieces bone in, skin on chicken (chicken legs or breasts, or a combination)
- 2 Oranges, unpeeled, sliced
- 1 lime, thinly sliced (optional)

How to Make

1. Make the marinade. In a large bowl or deep dish, mix together the first six ingredients: olive oil, white wine, orange juice, lime juice, mustard and brown sugar.
2. In a small bowl, mix together the spices: turmeric, garlic powder, coriander, paprika , salt and pepper. Now, add about half of the spice mix to the liquid marinade. Mix to combine.
3. Pat the chicken pieces dry and generously season with the remainder of the spice mix. Be sure to lift the chicken skins slightly and apply some of the spice mix underneath the skin.
4. Add the seasoned chicken and the remaining ingredients to the large bowl of marinade.
5. Work the chicken well into the marinade. Cover and refrigerate for 1-2 hours.
6. When ready, preheat the oven to 475 degrees F.
7. Transfer the chicken along with the marinade and everything else to a large baking pan so that everything is comfortably arranged in one layer. Be sure the chicken skin is facing up. Sprinkle with a dash or salt and more brown sugar, if you like.
8. Roast for 40-45 minutes, or until the chicken is cooked through and the chicken skin has nicely browned. Internal chicken temperature should be 170 degrees F. ▯

4-Weeks Exercise Program for Anti-Inflammatory Diet

When it comes to reducing inflammation, we often turn to a healthy diet, hot baths, and nourishing massages. While there's nothing wrong with beating inflammation using these tactics, exercise is also an effective way to lower inflammation. But when it comes to lowering inflammation, which types of exercise are best? Here's are the physical activity that can reduce inflammation:

Go for a Walk

When your body is inflamed, whether it's from intense exercise or something else, a light walk is an excellent way to reset. "Walking is a great way to let your muscles recover—it brings down inflammation by sending fresh blood and oxygen throughout your body, pumping the lymphatic system for waste removal, and gently restoring your digestive system if it feels off."

Hike

Want to take your walk to the next level? Immerse yourself in nature and go for a hike. "Find a safe trail, bring a friend, and go on an easy one-hour ramble through the woods. As an added bonus, 'forest bathing,' or time spent surrounded by trees, lowers the body's cortisol stress-response which is linked to inflammation by up to 20 percent."

Foam Roll

While it does have core-strengthening benefits, foam rolling is often considered a recovery tactic, and for good reason: It helps with muscle soreness, improves flexibility, improves sleep, helps with digestion, and lowers inflammation. "To reduce inflammation with a foam roller, lie on a roller and use gravity to apply pressure to a muscle. The roller is pressed into the muscle belly, and the user rolls up and down the length of the target muscle.

Do Yoga, Meditate, And Deep Breathe

This one probably doesn't come as much of a surprise, but the power of deep breathing and yoga as an inflammation-busting tactic can't be underestimated. "Deep, controlled breathing and meditation induce a state of physical and mental relaxation. This is incredibly helpful when you want to lower inflammation in the body." If you need ideas for specific yoga poses that lower inflammation, check out three of them here.

Daily physical activity has many benefits, such as controlling weight, strengthening the muscles, and reducing the risk of certain diseases. And regular participation in moderate-intensity exercise may enhance certain aspects of the immune system in addition to its anti-inflammatory properties. These effects are believed to reduce infection and lower the risk of cardiovascular disease. Here is a 4-Week exercise program to support your anti-inflammatory diet:

4-Week Plan Overview – Exercise to Reduce Whole Body Inflammation

WEEK	DAY 1	DAT 2	DAY 3	DAY 4	DAY 5	DAY 6	DAY 7
1	Aerobic Exercise 30 minutes	Light Circuit 15/20/15	Moderate Exercise 30 minutes	Rest	Moderate Exercise 30 minutes	Light Circuit 15/20/15	Rest
2	Aerobic Exercise 30 minutes	Light Circuit 15/20/15	Moderate Exercise 30 minutes	Rest	Moderate Exercise 30 minutes	Light Circuit 15/20/15	Rest
3	Aerobic Exercise 30 minutes	Moderate Circuit 15/20/15	Moderate Exercise 30 minutes	Rest	Vigorous Exercise 30 minutes	Light Circuit 15/20/15	Rest

4	Aerobic Exercise 30 minutes	Moderate Circuit 15/20/15	Moderate Exercise 30 minutes	Rest	Vigorous Exercise 30 minutes	Moderate Circuit 15/20/15	Rest

According to the anti-inflammatory diet and exercise program, working out four to five times a week with three days of aerobic exercise (walking, running, using the elliptical) and two days of circuit training or weight training can make the connection between exercise and inflammation, and it can significantly reduce inflammatory messengers and whole-body inflammation.

Note the workout regime has a good mixture of activities and rest periods so that your body has time to take a break in between vigorous exercise days.

Getting your heartbeat to 50 to 75 percent of its maximum rate for up to 30 minutes can help get you moving in the right direction. And knowing the benefits of exercise can help you motivate yourself to stick to this plan.

53689051R00188

Made in the USA
San Bernardino, CA
16 September 2019